COMPLETE WORKS

OF

EDGAR ALLAN POE

VOLUME 1

Illustrated Restored

Special Edition

Complete Works of
Edgar Allan Poe Volume 1:
Illustrated Restored Special Edition

Written by Edgar Allan Poe
Cover design by Mark Bussler

More books at
CGRpublishing.com

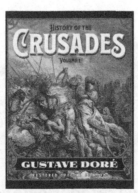

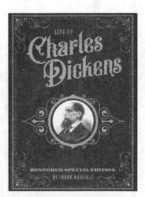

Best of Gustave Doré Volume 1: Illustrations from History's Most Versatile Artist

History of the Crusades Volumes 1 & 2: Gustave Doré Restored Special Edition

Life of Charles Dickens: Restored Special Edition

COMPLETE WORKS

of

Edgar Allan Poe

10 VOLUMES

VOLUME I.

POEMS

ESSAYS ON THE POET'S ART

NEW YORK

And the voice seemed his who fell in the battle down the dell and who is happy now

Bridal Ballad.

" And the voice seemed his who fell
In the battle down the dell,
    And who is happy now."

Contents

		PAGE
Edgar Allan Poe, World-Author, by Charles F. Richardson		325
Tamerlane		11
To —— ——		21
Dreams		22
Spirits of the Dead		24
Evening Star		26
A Dream Within a Dream		28
"In Youth have I Known One with whom the Earth"		30
A Dream		32
"The Happiest Day, the Happiest Hour"		33
The Lake. To ——		35
Sonnet: To Science		37
Al Aaraaf		38
To the River ——		58
To ——		59
Romance		60
Fairy-Land		61

iii

Contents

	PAGE
To ——	63
Alone	64
To Helen	66
Lenore	67
The Valley of Unrest	69
The City in the Sea	71
The Sleeper	75
Israfel	78
The Coliseum	81
To One in Paradise	84
Hymn	86
To F——	87
To F——s S. O——d	88
Scenes from " Politian "	89
To Zante	114
Bridal Ballad	115
The Haunted Palace	117
Silence	120
The Conqueror Worm	121
Dreamland	124
The Raven	127
Eulalie	136
To M. L. S.	138
Ulalume	139
To —— ——	144
An Enigma	146
To Helen	148
A Valentine	151

Contents

		PAGE
The Bells	. . . .	153
Annabel Lee	. . . . . .	158
To My Mother	. . . . . .	161
For Annie	. . . .	162
Eldorado	. . . .	168

THE POET'S ART

The Purpose of Poetry. Letter to B——	. .	171
The Poetic Principle	. . . . .	182
The Rationale of Verse	. . . .	216
Notes on English Verse	. . . .	285
The Philosophy of Composition	. . .	305

POEMS

TAMERLANE

" I wrapped myself in grandeur then
And donned a visionary crown."

Tamerlane

KIND solace in a dying hour,
    Such, father, is not now my theme;
    I will not madly deem that power
  Of earth may shrive me of the sin
  Unearthly pride hath revelled in;
  I have no time to dote or dream;
You call it hope, that fire of fire!
It is but agony of desire;
If I can hope—O God! I can—
  Its fount is holier, more divine.
I would not call thee fool, old man,
  But such is not a gift of thine.

Know thou the secret of a spirit
  Bowed from its wild pride into shame.
O yearning heart, I did inherit
  Thy withering portion with the fame,
The searing glory which hath shone
Amid the jewels of my throne,

Tamerlane

Halo of hell! and with a pain
Not hell shall make me fear again,
O craving heart, for the lost flowers
And sunshine of my summer hours!
The undying voice of that dead time,
With its interminable chime,
Rings, in the spirit of a spell,
Upon thy emptiness, a knell.

I have not always been as now;
The fevered diadem on my brow
    I claimed and won usurpingly.
Hath not the same fierce heirdom given
    Rome to the Cæsar, this to me?
        The heritage of a kingly mind,
And a proud spirit which hath striven
        Triumphantly with human kind.

On mountain soil I first drew life:
    The mists of the Taglay have shed
    Nightly their dews upon my head,
And I believe the wingèd strife
And tumult of the headlong air
Have nestled in my very hair.

So late from heaven, that dew, it fell
    ('Mid dreams of an unholy night)
Upon me with the touch of hell,
    While the red flashing of the light

Tamerlane

From clouds that hung, like banners, o'er,
　　Appeared to my half-closing eye
　　The pageantry of monarchy,
And the deep trumpet-thunder's roar
　　Came hurriedly upon me, telling
　　　　Of human battle, where my voice,
　　　　My own voice, silly child! was swelling
　　　　　(Oh! how my spirit would rejoice,
And leap within me at the cry)
The battle-cry of victory!

The rain came down upon my head
　　Unsheltered, and the heavy wind
　　Rendered me mad and deaf and blind.
It was but man, I thought, who shed
　　Laurels upon me; and the rush,
The torrent of the chilly air
　　Gurgled within my ear the crush
Of empires, with the captive's prayer,
The hum of suitors, and the tone
Of flattery round a sovereign's throne.

My passions, from that hapless hour,
　　Usurped a tyranny which men
Have deemed, since I have reached to power,
　　　　My innate nature; be it so;
　　But, father, there lived one who, then,
Then, in my boyhood, when their fire

Tamerlane

Burned with a still intenser glow
(For passion must, with youth, expire)
   E'en then who knew this iron heart
   In woman's weakness had a part.

I have no words, alas! to tell
The loveliness of loving well!
Nor would I now attempt to trace
The more than beauty of a face
Whose lineaments, upon my mind,
Are shadows on the unstable wind:
Thus I remember having dwelt
   Some page of early lore upon,
With loitering eye, till I have felt
The letters, with their meaning, melt
   To fantasies with none.

Oh, she was worthy of all love!
   Love, as in infancy, was mine;
'T was such as angel minds above
   Might envy; her young heart the shrine
On which my every hope and thought
   Were incense, then a goodly gift,
     For they were childish and upright,
Pure as her young example taught;
   Why did I leave it, and, adrift,
     Trust to the fire within for light?

Tamerlane

We grew in age, and love, together,
  Roaming the forest and the wild;
My breast her shield in wintry weather;
  And when the friendly sunshine smiled,
And she would mark the opening skies,
I saw no heaven but in her eyes.

Young love's first lesson is the heart;
  For 'mid that sunshine and those smiles,
When, from our little cares apart,
  And laughing at her girlish wiles,
I 'd throw me on her throbbing breast,
  And pour my spirit out in tears,
There was no need to speak the rest,
  No need to quiet any fears
Of her, who ask'd no reason why,
But turned on me her quiet eye.

Yet more than worthy of the love
My spirit struggled with, and strove,
When, on the mountain peak, alone,
Ambition lent it a new tone,
I had no being but in thee;
  The world, and all it did contain
In the earth, the air, the sea,
  Its joy, its little lot of pain
That was new pleasure, the ideal
  Dim vanities of dreams by night,

Tamerlane

And dimmer nothings which were real,
    (Shadows, and a more shadowy light!)
Parted upon their misty wings,
        And so, confusedly, became
        Thine image and a name, a name,
Two separate yet most intimate things.

I was ambitious; have you known
    The passion, father? You have not;
A cottager, I marked a throne
Of half the world as all my own,
    And murmured at such lowly lot;
But, just like any other dream,
    Upon the vapor of the dew
My own had passed, did not the beam
    Of beauty which did while it through
The minute, the hour, the day, oppress
My mind with double loveliness.

We walked together on the crown
Of a high mountain which looked down
Afar from its proud natural towers
    Of rock and forest on the hills—
The dwindled hills! begirt with bowers
    And shouting with a thousand rills.

I spoke to her of power and pride,
    But mystically, in such guise

Tamerlane

That she might deem it nought beside
   The moment's converse; in her eyes
I read, perhaps too carelessly,
   A mingled feeling with my own;
The flush on her bright cheek to me
   Seemed to become a queenly throne
Too well that I should let it be
   Light in the wilderness alone.

I wrapped myself in grandeur then,
   And donned a visionary crown;
     Yet it was not that Fantasy
     Had thrown her mantle over me,
But that, among the rabble—men,
   Lion ambition is chained down,
And crouches to a keeper's hand;
Not so in deserts where the grand,
The wild, the terrible, conspire
With their own breath to fan his fire.

Look round thee now on Samarcand!
   Is she not queen of Earth? her pride
Above all cities? in her hand
   Their destinies? in all beside
Of glory which the world hath known,
Stands she not nobly and alone?
Falling, her veriest stepping-stone
Shall form the pedestal of a throne!

Tamerlane

And who her sovereign?   Timour—he
  Whom the astonished people saw
Striding o'er empires haughtily
  A diademed outlaw!

O human love! thou spirit given
On earth of all we hope in heaven!
Which fall'st into the soul like rain
Upon the siroc-withered plain,
And, failing in thy power to bless,
But leav'st the heart a wilderness!
Idea! which bindest life around
With music of so strange a sound
And beauty of so wild a birth,
Farewell! for I have won the earth.

When Hope, the eagle that towered, could see
  No cliff beyond him in the sky,
His pinions were bent droopingly,
  And homeward turned his softened eye.
'T was sunset; when the sun will part
There comes a sullenness of heart
To him who still would look upon
The glory of the summer sun.
That soul will hate the evening mist,
So often lovely, and will list
To the sound of the coming darkness (known
To those whose spirits hearken) as one

Tamerlane

Who, in a dream of night, would fly,
But cannot from a danger nigh.

What though the moon, the white moon,
Shed all the splendor of her noon,
Her smile is chilly, and her beam,
In that time of dreariness, will seem
(So like you gather in your breath)
A portrait taken after death.
And boyhood is a summer sun
Whose waning is the dreariest one,
For all we live to know is known,
And all we seek to keep hath flown;
Let life, then, as the day-flower, fall
With the noonday beauty, which is all.

I reached my home, my home no more,
   For all had flown who made it so.
I passed from out its mossy door,
   And, though my tread was soft and low,
A voice came from the threshold stone
Of one whom I had earlier known.
   Oh, I defy thee, Hell, to show
   On beds of fire that burn below,
   An humbler heart, a deeper woe.

Father, I firmly do believe—
   I know, for Death who comes for me

Tamerlane

From regions of the blest afar,
Where there is nothing to deceive,
    Hath left his iron gate ajar,
And rays of truth you cannot see
Are flashing through eternity—
I do believe that Eblis hath
A snare in every human path;
Else how, when in the holy grove
I wandered of the idol, Love,
Who daily scents his snowy wings
With incense of burnt offerings
From the most unpolluted things,
Whose pleasant bowers are yet so riven
Above with trellised rays from heaven
No mote may shun, no tiniest fly,
The lightning of his eagle eye,
How was it that Ambition crept,
    Unseen, amid the revels there,
Till, growing bold, he laughed and leapt
    In the tangles of Love's very hair?

To —— ——

I SAW thee on thy bridal day,
　　When a burning blush came o'er thee,
　　Though happiness around thee lay,
　The world all love before thee;

And in thine eye a kindling light
　(Whatever it might be)
Was all on earth my aching sight
　Of loveliness could see.

That blush, perhaps, was maiden shame;
　As such it well may pass;
Though its glow hath raised a fiercer flame
　In the breast of him, alas!

Who saw thee on that bridal day,
　When that deep blush would come o'er thee,
Though happiness around thee lay,
　The world all love before thee.

Dreams

OH that my young life were a lasting dream,
    My spirit not awakening till the beam
    Of an eternity should bring the morrow!
Yes, though that long dream were of hopeless sorrow,
'T were better than the cold reality
Of waking life to him whose heart must be,
And hath been still, upon the lovely earth,
A chaos of deep passion from his birth.
But should it be—that dream eternally
Continuing, as dreams have been to me
In my young boyhood—should it thus be given,
'T were folly still to hope for higher heaven.
For I have revelled, when the sun was bright
I' the summer sky, in dreams of living light
And loveliness; have left my very heart
In climes of mine imagining, apart
From mine own home, with beings that have been
Of mine own thought—what more could I have seen?
'T was once, and only once, and the wild hour

Dreams

From my remembrance shall not pass—some power
Or spell had bound me—'t was the chilly wind
Came o'er me in the night and left behind
Its image on my spirit, or the moon
Shone on my slumbers in her lofty noon
Too coldly, or the stars—howe'er it was,
That dream was as that night-wind—let it pass.

I have been happy, though [but] in a dream.
I have been happy, and I love the theme;
Dreams! in their vivid coloring of life,
As in that fleeting, shadowy, misty strife
Of semblance with reality which brings
To the delirious eye more lovely things
Of paradise and love—and all our own!—
Than young Hope in his sunniest hour hath known.

Spirits of the Dead

THY soul shall find itself alone
    'Mid dark thoughts of the gray tombstone;
    Not one of all the crowd, to pry
Into thine hour of secrecy.

Be silent in that solitude
    Which is not loneliness, for then
The spirits of the dead who stood
    In life before thee are again
In death around thee, and their will
Shall overshadow thee; be still.

The night, though clear, shall frown,
And the stars shall not look down
From their high thrones in the heaven
With light like hope to mortals given;
But their red orbs, without beam,
To thy weariness shall seem

Spirits of the Dead

As a burning and a fever
Which would cling to thee forever.
Now are thoughts thou shalt not banish;
Now are visions ne'er to vanish;
From thy spirit shall they pass
No more, like dew-drops from the grass.

The breeze, the breath of God, is still,
And the mist upon the hill
Shadowy, shadowy, yet unbroken,
Is a symbol and a token;
How it hangs upon the trees,
A mystery of mysteries!

Evening Star

'TWAS noontide of summer
      And mid-time of night;
      And stars, in their orbits,
   Shone pale through the light
Of the brighter cold moon,
   'Mid planets her slaves,
Herself in the heavens,
   Her beam on the waves.
      I gazed awhile
      On her cold smile,
Too cold, too cold for me;
   There passed, as a shroud,
   A fleecy cloud,
And I turned away to thee,
   Proud evening star,
   In thy glory afar,
And dearer thy beam shall be;
   For joy to my heart
   Is the proud part

Evening Star

Thou bearest in heaven at night,
And more I admire
Thy distant fire
Than that colder, lowly light.

A Dream Within a Dream

TAKE this kiss upon the brow!
　　And, in parting from you now,
　　Thus much let me avow:
You are not wrong, who deem
That my days have been a dream;
Yet if hope has flown away
In a night, or in a day,
In a vision, or in none,
Is it therefore the less gone?
All that we see or seem
Is but a dream within a dream.

I stand amid the roar
Of a surf-tormented shore,
And I hold within my hand
Grains of the golden sand—
How few! yet how they creep
Through my fingers to the deep,

A Dream within a Dream

While I weep, while I weep!
O God! can I not grasp
Them with a tighter clasp?
O God! can I not save
One from the pitiless wave?
Is all that we see or seem
But a dream within a dream?

"In Youth have I Known One with whom the Earth"

How often we forget all time, when lone
Admiring Nature's universal throne;
Her woods, her wilds, her mountains, the intense
Reply of hers to our intelligence!

I

IN youth have I known one with whom the
earth
    In secret communing held, as he with it,
In daylight and in beauty from his birth;
   Whose fervid, flickering torch of life was lit
From the sun and stars, whence he had drawn forth
   A passionate light—such for his spirit was fit;
And yet that spirit knew not, in the hour
Of its own fervor, what had o'er it power.

2

Perhaps it may be that my mind is wrought
   To a fever by the moonbeam that hangs o'er,

"In Youth Have I Known One"

But I will half believe that wild light fraught
   With more of sovereignty than ancient lore
Hath ever told; or is it of a thought
   The unembodied essence and no more,
That with a quickening spell doth o'er us pass
As dew of the night-time o'er the summer grass?

3

Doth o'er us pass, when, as the expanding eye
   To the loved object, so the tear to the lid
Will start, which lately slept in apathy.
   And yet it need not be—that object—hid
From us in life, but common—which doth lie
   Each hour before us—but then only bid
With a strange sound, as of a harp-string broken,
To awake us. 'T is a symbol and a token

4

Of what in other worlds shall be, and given
   In beauty by our God to those alone
Who otherwise would fall from life and heaven,
   Drawn by their heart's passion, and that tone,
That high tone of the spirit which hath striven
   Though not with faith, with godliness, whose throne
With desperate energy 't hath beaten down;
Wearing its own deep feeling as a crown.

A Dream

IN visions of the dark night
    I have dreamed of joy departed;
    But a waking dream of life and light
Hath left me broken-hearted.

Ah! what is not a dream by day
    To him whose eyes are cast
On things around him, with a ray
    Turned back upon the past?

That holy dream, that holy dream,
    While all the world were chiding,
Hath cheered me as a lovely beam
    A lonely spirit guiding.

What though that light, through storm and night,
    So trembled from afar,
What could there be more purely bright
    In Truth's day-star?

"The Happiest Day, the Happiest Hour"

THE happiest day, the happiest hour
    My seared and blighted heart hath known,
The highest hope of pride and power,
  I feel hath flown.

Of power, said I?   Yes, such I ween;
  But they have vanished long, alas!
The visions of my youth have been—
  But let them pass.

And pride, what have I now with thee?
  Another brow may even inherit
The venom thou hast poured on me;
  Be still, my spirit!

The happiest day, the happiest hour
  Mine eyes shall see—have ever seen,

" The Happiest Day, the Happiest Hour "

The brightest glance of pride and power,
   I feel have been;

But were that hope of pride and power
   Now offered with the pain
Even then I felt, that brightest hour
   I would not live again.

For on its wing was dark alloy,
   And, as it fluttered, fell
An essence powerful to destroy
   A soul that knew it well.

The Lake. To ——

I**N** spring of youth it was my lot
To haunt of the wide world a spot
The which I could not love the less,
So lovely was the loneliness
Of a wild lake, with black rock bound,
And the tall pines that towered around.

But when the night had thrown her pall
Upon that spot, as upon all,
And the mystic wind went by,
Murmuring in melody,
Then, ah! then I would awake
To the terror of the lone lake.

Yet that terror was not fright,
But a tremulous delight;

The Lake.   To ———

A feeling not the jewelled mine
Could teach or bribe me to define,
Nor love, although the love were thine.

Death was in that poisonous wave,
And in its gulf a fitting grave
For him who thence could solace bring
To his lone imagining—
Whose solitary soul could make
An Eden of that dim lake.

Sonnet: To Science

SCIENCE! true daughter of old Time thou art,
    Who alterest all things with thy peering
      eyes.
Why preyest thou thus upon the poet's heart,
    Vulture, whose wings are dull realities?
How should he love thee, or how deem thee wise,
    Who wouldst not leave him in his wandering
To seek for treasure in the jewelled skies,
    Albeit he soared with an undaunted wing?
Hast thou not dragged Diana from her car,
    And driven the hamadryad from the wood
To seek a shelter in some happier star?
    Hast thou not torn the naiad from her flood,
The elfin from the green grass, and from me
The summer dream beneath the tamarind tree?

Al Aaraaf [1]

PART I

OH! nothing earthly save the ray
    (Thrown back from flowers) of Beauty's eye,
    As in those gardens where the day
  Springs from the gems of Circassy:
Oh! nothing earthly save the thrill
Of melody in woodland rill;
Or (music of the passion-hearted)
Joy's voice so peacefully departed
That, like the murmur in the shell,
Its echo dwelleth and will dwell:
Oh! nothing of the dross of ours,
Yet all the beauty, all the flowers
That list our love and deck our bowers
Adorn yon world afar, afar,
The wandering star.

[1] A star was discovered by Tycho Brahe, which appeared suddenly in the heavens, attained in a few days a brilliancy surpassing that of Jupiter, then as suddenly disappeared, and has never been seen since.

Al Aaraaf

'T was a sweet time for Nesace; for there
Her world lay lolling on the golden air,
Near four bright suns, a temporary rest,
An oasis in desert of the blest.
Away, away, 'mid seas of rays that roll
Empyrean splendor o'er the unchained soul,—
The soul that scarce (the billows are so dense)
Can struggle to its destined eminence,—
To distant spheres, from time to time, she rode
And late to ours, the favored one of God;
But now, the ruler of an anchor'd realm,
She throws aside the sceptre, leaves the helm,
And, amid incense and high spiritual hymns,
Laves in quadruple light her angel limbs.

Now happiest, loveliest in yon lovely earth,
Whence sprang the " Idea of Beauty " into birth
(Falling in wreaths through many a startled star,
Like woman's hair 'mid pearls, until, afar,
It lit on hills Achaian and there dwelt),
She look'd into infinity, and knelt.
Rich clouds, for canopies, about her curled,
Fit emblems of the model of her world,
Seen but in beauty, not impeding sight
Of other beauty glittering through the light—
A wreath that twined each starry form around,
And all the opaled air in color bound.

Al Aaraaf

All hurriedly she knelt upon a bed
Of flowers: of lilies such as reared the head
On the fair Capo Deucato,[1] and sprang
So eagerly around about to hang
Upon the flying footsteps of—deep pride—
Of her who loved a mortal [2]—and so died.
The Sephalica, budding with young bees,
Upreared its purple stem around her knees;
And gemmy flower,[3] of Trebizond misnamed,
Inmate of highest stars, where erst it shamed
All other loveliness; its honeyed dew,
(The fabled nectar that the heathen knew)
Deliriously sweet, was dropped from heaven,
And fell on gardens of the unforgiven
In Trebizond, and on a sunny flower
So like its own above that, to this hour,
It still remaineth, torturing the bee
With madness and unwonted revery.
In heaven and all its environs the leaf
And blossom of the fairy plant in grief
Disconsolate linger—grief that hangs her head,
Repenting follies that full long have fled,
Heaving her white breast to the balmy air,
Like guilty beauty, chastened, and more fair:

---

[1] On Santa Maura—olim Deucadia.
[2] Sappho.
[3] This flower is much noticed by Lewenhoeck and Tournefort. The bee
feeding upon its blossom becomes intoxicated.

AL AARAAF

"All hurriedly she knelt upon a bed
    Of flowers: of lilies such as reared the head
    On the fair Capo Deucato."

Al Aaraaf

Nyctanthes too, as sacred as the light
She fears to perfume, perfuming the night;
And Clytia[1] pondering between many a sun,
While pettish tears adown her petals run;
And that aspiring flower[2] that sprang on earth
And died, ere scarce exalted into birth,
Bursting its odorous heart in spirit to wing
Its way to heaven, from garden of a king;
And Valisnerian lotus[3] thither flown
From struggling with the waters of the Rhone;
And thy most lovely purple perfume, Zante![4]
Isola d' oro!   Fior di Levante!
And the Nelumbo bud[5] that floats forever
With Indian Cupid down the holy river—
Fair flowers, and fairy! to whose care is given
To bear the goddess' song in odors up to heaven:[6]

---

[1] Clytia: the Chrysanthemum Peruvianum, or, to employ a better-known term, the turnsol, which turns continually toward the sun, covers itself, like Peru, the country from which it comes, with dewy clouds which cool and refresh its flowers during the most violent heat of the day.—*B. de St. Pierre.*

[2] There is cultivated in the king's garden at Paris, a species of serpentine aloes without prickles, whose large and beautiful flower exhales a strong odor of the vanilla, during the time of its expansion, which is very short.   It does not blow till toward the month of July; you then perceive it gradually open its petals, expand them, fade, and die.—*St. Pierre.*

[3] There is found, in the Rhone, a beautiful lily of the Valisnerian kind. Its stem will stretch to the length of three or four feet, thus preserving its head above water in the swellings of the river.

[4] The hyacinth.

[5] It is a fiction of the Indians that Cupid was first seen floating in one of these down the river Ganges, and that he loves the cradle of his childhood.

[6] And golden vials full of odors, which are the prayers of saints.—*Rev. St John.*

Al Aaraaf

" Spirit! that dwellest where,

    In the deep sky,

The terrible and fair

    In beauty vie!

Beyond the line of blue,

    The boundary of the star

Which turneth at the view

    Of thy barrier and thy bar,—

Of the barrier overgone

    By the comets who were cast

From their pride and from their throne

    To be drudges till the last,

To be carriers of fire

    (The red fire of their heart)

With speed that may not tire

    And with pain that shall not part,

Who livest—that we know,

    In eternity—we feel,

But the shadow of whose brow

    What spirit shall reveal?

Though the beings whom thy Nesace,

    Thy messenger, hath known

Have dreamed for thy infinity

    A model of their own,[1]

[1] The Humanitarians held that God was to be understood as having really a human form.—*Vide Clarke's Sermons,* vol. i., page 26, fol. edit.

The drift of Milton's argument leads him to employ language which would appear, at first sight, to verge upon their doctrine; but it will be seen immediately that he guards himself against the charge of having adopted one of

Al Aaraaf

Thy will is done, O God!
   The star hath ridden high
Through many a tempest, but she rode
   Beneath thy burning eye;
And here, in thought, to thee—
   In thought that can alone
Ascend thy empire, and so be
   A partner of thy throne—
By winged Fantasy [1]
   My embassy is given,
Till secrecy shall knowledge be
   In the environs of heaven."

She ceased; and buried then her burning cheek
Abashed, amid the lilies there, to seek
A shelter from the fervor of His eye;
For the stars trembled at the Deity.
She stirred not, breathed not, for a voice was there

---

the most ignorant errors of the dark ages of the church.—*Dr. Summer's Notes on Milton's Christian Doctrine.*

This opinion, in spite of many testimonies to the contrary, could never have been very general. Audeus, a Syrian of Mesopotamia, was condemned for the opinion as heretical. He lived in the beginning of the fourth century. His disciples were called Anthropomorphites.—*Vide Du Pin.*

Among Milton's minor poems are these lines:

> Dicite sacrorum præsides nemorum Deæ, &c.
> Quis ille primus cujus ex imagine
> Natura solers finxit humanum genus?
> Eternus, incorruptus, æquævus polo,
> Unusque et universus exemplar Dei.

And afterward:

> Non cui profundum Cæcitas lumen dedit
> Dircæus augur vidit hunc alto sinu, &c.

[1] Seltsumen Tochter Jovis
Seinem Schosskinde
Der Phantasie.—*Goethe.*

Al Aaraaf

How solemnly pervading the calm air!
A sound of silence on the startled ear
Which dreamy poets name "the music of the sphere."
Ours is a world of words; quiet we call
" Silence," which is the merest word of all.
All Nature speaks, and even ideal things
Flap shadowy sounds from visionary wings;
But ah! not so when, thus, in realms on high
The eternal voice of God is passing by,
And the red winds are withering in the sky:—

" What though in worlds which sightless cycles run,[1]
Linked to a little system, and one sun—
Where all my love is folly and the crowd
Still think my terrors but the thunder cloud,
The storm, the earthquake, and the ocean-wrath—
(Ah! will they cross me in my angrier path?)
What though in worlds which own a single sun
The sands of time grow dimmer as they run,
Yet thine is my resplendency, so given
To bear my secrets through the upper heaven.
Leave tenantless thy crystal home, and fly,
With all thy train, athwart the moony sky,
Apart, like fireflies[2] in Sicilian night,

---

[1] Sightless—too small to be seen.—*Legge*.

[2] I have often noticed a peculiar movement of the fireflies: they will collect in a body and fly off, from a common centre, into innumerable radii.

Al Aaraaf

And wing to other worlds another light!
Divulge the secrets of thy embassy
To the proud orbs that twinkle, and so be
To every heart a barrier and a ban
Lest the stars totter in the guilt of man!"

Up rose the maiden in the yellow night,
The single-moonèd eve! On earth we plight
Our faith to one love, and one moon adore;
The birthplace of young Beauty had no more.
As sprang that yellow star from downy hours
Up rose the maiden from her shrine of flowers,
And bent o'er sheeny mountain and dim plain
Her way—but left not yet her Therasæan reign.[1]

PART II

HIGH on a mountain of enamelled head,—
Such as the drowsy shepherd on his bed
Of giant pasturage lying at his ease,
Raising his heavy eyelid, starts and sees
With many a muttered " hope to be forgiven,"
What time the moon is quadrated in heaven,—
Of rosy head that, towering far away
Into the sunlit ether, caught the ray

---

[1] Therasæa, or Therasea, the island mentioned by Seneca, which, in a
moment, arose from the sea to the eyes of astonished mariners.

Al Aaraaf

Of sunken suns at eve, at noon of night,
While the moon danced with the fair stranger light,
Upreared upon such height arose a pile
Of gorgeous columns on the unburthened air,
Flashing from Parian marble that twin smile
Far down upon the wave that sparkled there,
And nursled the young mountain in its lair.
Of molten stars their pavement, such as fall [1]
Through the ebon air, besilvering the pall
Of their own dissolution, while they die,
Adorning then the dwellings of the sky.
A dome, by linked light from heaven let down,
Sat gently on these columns as a crown;
A window of one circular diamond, there,
Looked out above into the purple air,
And rays from God shot down that meteor chain
And hallowed all the beauty twice again,
Save when, between the empyrean and that ring,
Some eager spirit flapped his dusky wing.
But on the pillars seraph eyes have seen
The dimness of this world; that grayish green
That Nature loves the best for Beauty's grave
Lurked in each cornice, round each architrave;
And every sculptured cherub thereabout,
That from his marble dwelling peerèd out,
Seemed earthly in the shadow of his niche—

---

[1] Some star which, from the ruin'd roof
Of shak'd Olympus, by mischance, did fall.—*Milton.*

Al Aaraaf

Achaian statues in a world so rich!
Friezes from Tadmor and Persepolis,[1]
From Baalbek, and the stilly, clear abyss
Of beautiful Gomorrah! Oh! the wave[2]
Is now upon thee, but too late to save!

Sound loves to revel in a summer night:
Witness the murmur of the gray twilight
That stole upon the ear, in Eyraco,[3]
Of many a wild star-gazer long ago;
That stealeth ever on the ear of him
Who, musing, gazeth on the distance dim,
And sees the darkness coming as a cloud;
Is not its form, its voice,[4] most palpable and loud?

But what is this? it cometh, and it brings
A music with it; 't is the rush of wings;

---

[1] Voltaire, in speaking of Persepolis, says: " Je connois bien l'admiration qu' inspirent ces ruines—mais un palais érigé au pied d'une chaine des rochers sterils—peut il être un chef-d'œuvre des arts? "

[2] " Oh! the wave "—Ula Deguisi is the Turkish appellation; but, on its own shores, it is called Bahar Loth, or Almotanah. There were undoubtedly more than two cities engulfed in the " Dead Sea." In the valley of Siddim were five—Admah, Zeboim, Zoar, Sodom, and Gomorrah. Stephen of Byzantium mentions eight, and Strabo thirteen (engulfed), but the last is out of all reason.

It is said (Tacitus, Strabo, Josephus, Daniel of St. Saba, Nau, Mundrell, Troilo, D'Arvieux) that after an excessive drought the vestiges of columns, walls, etc., are seen above the surface. At any season, such remains may be discovered by looking down into the transparent lake, and at such distances as would argue the existence of many settlements in the space now usurped by the "Asphaltites."

[3] Eyraco—Chaldea.

[4] I have often thought I could distinctly hear the sound of the darkness as it stole over the horizon.

Al Aaraaf

A pause, and then a sweeping, falling strain,
And Nesace is in her halls again.
From the wild energy of wanton haste
  Her cheeks were flushing and her lips apart;
And zone that clung around her gentle waist
  Had burst beneath the heaving of her heart.
Within the centre of that hall to breathe
She paused and panted, Zanthe! all beneath
The fairy light that kiss'd her golden hair
And longed to rest, yet could but sparkle there!

  Young flowers were whispering in melody
To happy flowers that night,[1] and tree to tree;
Fountains were gushing music as they fell
In many a starlit grove or moonlit dell;
Yet silence came upon material things,
Fair flowers, bright waterfalls, and angel wings;
And sound alone that from the spirit sprang
Bore burthen to the charm the maiden sang:

    " 'Neath blue-bell or streamer
      Or tufted wild spray
    That keeps, from the dreamer,
      The moonbeam away[2]—

---

[1] Fairies use flowers for their charactery.—*Merry Wives of Windsor.*

[2] In Scripture is this passage—" The sun shall not harm thee by day, nor the moon by night." It is perhaps not generally known that the moon, in Egypt, has the effect of producing blindness to those who sleep with the face exposed to its rays, to which circumstance the passage evidently alludes.

Al Aaraaf

Bright beings, that ponder,
　　With half-closing eyes,
On the stars, which your wonder
　　Hath drawn from the skies,
Till they glance through the shade, and
　　Come down to your brow
Like eyes of the maiden
　　Who calls on you now,
Arise! from your dreaming
　　In violet bowers,
To duty beseeming
　　These starlitten hours,
And shake from your tresses,
　　Encumbered with dew,
The breath of those kisses
　　That cumber them too—
(Oh! how, without you, Love,
　　Could angels be blest?)
Those kisses of true love
　　That lulled ye to rest!
Up! shake from your wing
　　Each hindering thing:
The dew of the night—
　　It would weigh down your flight;
And true love caresses,
　　Oh! leave them apart!
They are light on the tresses,
　　But lead on the heart.

Al Aaraaf

" Ligeia! Ligeia!
  My beautiful one!
Whose harshest idea
  Will to melody run,
Oh! is it thy will
  On the breezes to toss?
Or, capriciously still,
  Like the lone albatross,[1]
Incumbent on night
  (As she on the air)
To keep watch with delight
  On the harmony there?

" Ligeia! wherever
  Thy image may be,
No magic shall sever
  Thy music from thee.
Thou hast bound many eyes
  In a dreamy sleep,
But the strains still arise
  Which thy vigilance keep:
The sound of the rain
  Which leaps down to the flower,
And dances again
  In the rhythm of the shower;
The murmur that springs
  From the growing of grass[2]

---

[1] The albatross is said to sleep on the wing.
[2] I met with this idea in an old English tale, which I am now unable to

Al Aaraaf

Are the music of things—
 But are modelled, alas!
Away, then, my dearest,
 Oh! hie thee away
To springs that lie clearest
 Beneath the moon-ray;
To lone lake that smiles,
 In its dream of deep rest,
At the many star-isles
 That enjewel its breast;
Where wild flowers, creeping,
 Have mingled their shade,
On its margin is sleeping
 Full many a maid;
Some have left the cool glade, and
 Have slept with the bee [1]—
Arouse them, my maiden,
 On moorland and lea;
Go! breathe on their slumber,
 All softly in ear,
The musical number

---

obtain, and quote from memory.—" The verie essence and, as it were, springe-heade and origine of all musicke is the verie pleasaunte sounde which the trees of the forest do make when they growe."

[1] The wild bee will not sleep in the shade if there be moonlight.

The rhyme in this verse, as in one about sixty lines before, has an appearance of affectation. It is, however, imitated from Sir W. Scott, or rather from Claud Halcro—in whose mouth I admired its effect:

> " Oh! were there an island,
> Tho' ever so wild,
> Where women might smile, and
> No man be beguiled," etc.

Al Aaraaf

They slumbered to hear;
For what can awaken
An angel so soon,
Whose sleep hath been taken
Beneath the cold moon,
As the spell which no slumber
Of witchery may test,
The rhythmical number
Which lulled him to rest ? "

Spirits in wing, and angels to the view,
A thousand seraphs burst the empyrean through,
Young dreams still hovering on their drowsy flight—
Seraphs in all but " knowledge," the keen light
That fell, refracted, through thy bounds, afar,
O Death! from eye of God upon that star.
Sweet was that error, sweeter still that death;
Sweet was that error—even with us the breath
Of Science dims the mirror of our joy;
To them 't were the simoom, and would destroy;
For what (to them) availeth it to know
That truth is falsehood—or that bliss is woe?
Sweet was their death; with them to die was rife
With the last ecstasy of satiate life;
Beyond that death no immortality,
But sleep that pondereth and is not " to be "—
And there, oh! may my weary spirit dwell,

Al Aaraaf

Apart from heaven's eternity, and yet how far from
    hell![1]
What guilty spirit, in what shrubbery dim,
Heard not the stirring summons of that hymn?
But two; they fell; for Heaven no grace imparts
To those who hear not for their beating hearts;
A maiden-angel and her seraph-lover.
Oh, where (and ye may seek the wide skies over)
Was Love, the blind, near sober Duty known?
Unguided Love hath fallen, 'mid " tears of perfect
    moan."[2]

He was a goodly spirit, he who fell:
A wanderer by mossy-mantled well,
A gazer on the lights that shine above,
A dreamer in the moonbeam by his love;
What wonder? for each star is eye-like there,

[1] With the Arabians there is a medium between heaven and hell, where
men suffer no punishment, but yet do not attain that tranquil and even happi-
ness which they suppose to be characteristic of heavenly enjoyment.

> Un no rompido sueno—
> Un dia puro—allegre—libre
> Quiera—
> Libre de amor—de zelo—
> De odio—de esperanza—de rezelo.—*Luis Ponce de Leon.*

Sorrow is not excluded from " Al Aaraaf," but it is that sorrow which the
living love to cherish for the dead, and which, in some minds, resembles the
delirium of opium. The passionate excitement of love and the buoyancy
of spirit attendant upon intoxication are its less holy pleasures, the price of
which, to those souls who make choice of " Al Aaraaf " as their residence
after life, is final death and annihilation.

> [2] There be tears of perfect moan
> Wept for thee in Helicon.—*Milton.*

Al Aaraaf

And looks so sweetly down on Beauty's hair;
And they, and every mossy spring, were holy
To his love-haunted heart and melancholy.
The night had found (to him a night of woe),
Upon a mountain crag, young Angelo;
Beetling it bends athwart the solemn sky,
And scowls on starry worlds that down beneath it lie.
Here sat he with his love, his dark eye bent
With eagle gaze along the firmament;
Now turned it upon her, but ever then
It trembled to the orb of earth again.

" Ianthe, dearest, see! how dim that ray!
How lovely 't is to look so far away!
She seemed not thus upon that autumn eve
I left her gorgeous halls, nor mourned to leave.
That eve, that eve, I should remember well,
The sun-ray dropped, in Lemnos, with a spell
On the arabesque carving of a gilded hall
Wherein I sat, and on the draperied wall;
And on my eyelids; oh, the heavy light,
How drowsily it weighed them into night!
On flowers before, and mist, and love they ran
With Persian Saadi in his Gulistan:
But oh, that light! I slumbered; Death, the while,
Stole o'er my senses in that lovely isle
So softly that no single silken hair
Awoke that slept, or knew that he was there.

Al Aaraaf

" The last spot of earth's orb I trod upon
Was a proud temple call'd the Parthenon.[1]
More beauty clung around her columned wall
Than even thy glowing bosom beats withal;[2]
And when old Time my wing did disenthral
Thence sprang I, as the eagle from his tower;
And years I left behind me in an hour.
What time upon her airy bounds I hung
One half the garden of her globe was flung,
Unrolling as a chart unto my view;
Tenantless cities of the desert too!
Ianthe, beauty crowded on me then,
And half I wished to be again of men.

" My Angelo! and why of them to be?
A brighter dwelling-place is here for thee,
And greener fields than in yon world above,
And woman's loveliness, and passionate love.

" But list, Ianthe! when the air so soft
Failed, as my pennon'd[3] spirit leapt aloft,
Perhaps my brain grew dizzy, but the world
I left so late was into chaos hurled,
Sprang from her station, on the winds apart,
And rolled, a flame, the fiery heaven athwart.
Methought, my sweet one, then I ceased to soar

---

[1] It was entire in 1687—the most elevated spot in Athens.
[2] Shadowing more beauty in their airy brows
   Than have the white breasts of the Queen of Love.—*Marlowe.*
[3] Pennon—for pinion.—*Milton.*

Al Aaraaf

And fell; not swiftly as I rose before,
But with a downward, tremulous motion through
Light, brazen rays this golden star unto!
Nor long the measure of my falling hours,
For nearest of all stars was thine to ours,
Dread star! that came, amid a night of mirth,
A red Dædalion on the timid earth.

" We came, and to thy earth ; but not to us
Be given our lady's bidding to discuss ;
We came, my love; around, above, below,
Gay firefly of the night we come and go,
Nor ask a reason save the angel-nod
She grants to us, as granted by her God.
But, Angelo, than thine gray Time unfurled
Never his fairy wing o'er fairer world!
Dim was its little disk, and angel eyes
Alone could see the phantom in the skies,
When first Al Aaraaf knew her course to be
Headlong thitherward o'er the starry sea;
But when its glory swelled upon the sky,
As glowing Beauty's bust beneath man's eye,
We paused before the heritage of men,
And thy star trembled, as doth Beauty then! "

Thus, in discourse, the lovers whiled away
The night that waned and waned and brought no day.
They fell; for Heaven to them no hope imparts
Who hear not for the beating of their hearts.

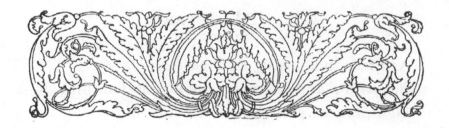

To the River ——

FAIR river! in thy bright, clear flow
　　Of crystal, wandering water,
　　Thou art an emblem of the glow
　Of beauty, the unhidden heart,
　The playful maziness of art
In old Alberto's daughter;

But when within thy wave she looks,
　Which glistens then, and trembles,
Why, then, the prettiest of brooks
　Her worshipper resembles;
For in his heart, as in thy stream,
　Her image deeply lies—
His heart which trembles at the beam
　Of her soul-searching eyes.

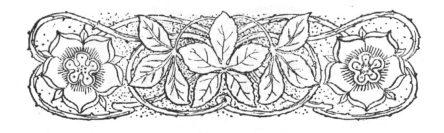

To ——

THE bowers whereat, in dreams, I see
　　The wantonest singing birds
　　Are lips, and all thy melody
Of lip-begotten words.

Thine eyes, in heaven of heart enshrined
　　Then desolately fall,
O God! on my funereal mind
　　Like starlight on a pall.

Thy heart, thy heart!　I wake and sigh,
　　And sleep to dream till day
Of the truth that gold can never buy—
　　Of the baubles that it may.

Romance

ROMANCE, who loves to nod and sing,
   With drowsy head and folded wing,
   Among the green leaves as they shake
Far down within some shadowy lake,
  To me a painted paroquet
Hath been—a most familiar bird;
  Taught me my alphabet to say,
To lisp my very earliest word
While in the wild wood I did lie,
A child, with a most knowing eye.

Of late, eternal condor years
  So shake the very heaven on high
  With tumult as they thunder by,
I have no time for idle cares
  Through gazing on the unquiet sky.
And when an hour with calmer wings
Its down upon my spirit flings,
That little time with lyre and rhyme
  To while away—forbidden things!
My heart would feel to be a crime
  Unless it trembled with the strings.

Fairy-Land

DIM vales, and shadowy floods,
   And cloudy-looking woods,
   Whose forms we can't discover
For the tears that drip all over!
Huge moons there wax and wane—
Again, again, again,
Every moment of the night
Forever changing places;
And they put out the starlight
With the breath from their pale faces.
About twelve by the moon-dial
One, more filmy than the rest,
(A kind which, upon trial,
They have found to be the best)
Comes down, still down, and down,
With its centre on the crown
Of a mountain's eminence,
While its wide circumference
In easy drapery falls

Fairy-Land

Over hamlets, over halls,
Wherever they may be;
O'er the strange woods, o'er the sea,
Over spirits on the wing,
Over every drowsy thing,
And buries them up quite
In a labyrinth of light;
And then, how deep, oh, deep,
Is the passion of their sleep!
In the morning they arise,
And their moony covering
Is soaring in the skies,
With the tempests as they toss,
Like——almost any thing—
Or a yellow albatross.
They use that moon no more
For the same end as before,
Videlicet, a tent,
Which I think extravagant.
Its atomies, however,
Into a shower dissever,
Of which those butterflies
Of earth, who seek the skies,
And so come down again
(Never-contented things!)
Have brought a specimen
Upon their quivering wings.

To ——

HEED not that my earthly lot
    Hath little of earth in it,
    That years of love have been forgot
  In the hatred of a minute;
I mourn not that the desolate
  Are happier, sweet, than I,
But that you sorrow for my fate
  Who am a passer-by.

Alone

FROM childhood's hour I have not been
    As others were; I have not seen
    As others saw; I could not bring
My passions from a common spring.
From the same source I have not taken
My sorrow; I could not awaken
My heart to joy at the same tone;
And all I loved, I loved alone.
Then, in my childhood, in the dawn
Of a most stormy life, was drawn
From every depth of good and ill
The mystery which binds me still:
From the torrent or the fountain;
From the red cliff of the mountain;

Alone

From the sun that round me rolled
In its autumn tint of gold;
From the lightning in the sky
As it passed me flying by;
From the thunder and the storm;
And the cloud that took the form
(When the rest of heaven was blue)
Of a demon in my view.

To Helen

HELEN, thy beauty is to me
    Like those Nicean barks of yore,
    That gently, o'er a perfumed sea,
The weary, wayworn wanderer bore
To his own native shore.

On desperate seas long wont to roam,
    Thy hyacinth hair, thy classic face,
Thy naiad airs have brought me home
    To the glory that was Greece
And the grandeur that was Rome.

Lo! in yon brilliant window-niche
    How statue-like I see thee stand,
    The agate lamp within thy hand,
Ah! Psyche, from the regions which
    Are Holy Land!

Lenore

A H, broken is the golden bowl! the spirit flown
    forever!
    Let the bell toll! a saintly soul floats on the
Stygian river;
And, Guy De Vere, hast thou no tear? weep now or
    never more!
See on yon drear and rigid bier low lies thy love, Lenore!
Come! let the burial rite be read, the funeral song be
    sung,
An anthem for the queenliest dead that ever died so
    young,
A dirge for her, the doubly dead in that she died so
    young.

" Wretches! ye loved her for her wealth and hated
    her for her pride,
And when she fell in feeble health, ye blessed her—
    that she died!
How shall the ritual, then, be read? the requiem how
    be sung

Lenore

By you, by yours, the evil eye, by yours, the slander-
  ous tongue
That did to death the innocence that died, and died so
  young ? "

Peccavímus; but rave not thus! and let a Sabbath song
Go up to God so solemnly the dead may feel no wrong!
The sweet Lenore hath gone before, with Hope, that
  flew beside,
Leaving thee wild for the dear child that should have
  been thy bride—
For her, the fair and debonair, that now so lowly lies,
The life upon her yellow hair but not within her eyes;
The life still there, upon her hair, the death upon her
  eyes.

" Avaunt! to-night my heart is light; no dirge will I
  upraise,
But waft the angel on her flight with a pæan of old
  days!
Let no bell toll! lest her sweet soul, amid its hallowed
  mirth,
Should catch the note, as it doth float up from the
  damnèd earth.
To friends above, from fiends below, the indignant
  ghost is riven,
From hell unto a high estate far up within the heaven—
From grief and groan to a golden throne, beside the
  King of heaven."

The Valley of Unrest

ONCE it smiled a silent dell
     Where the people did not dwell;
     They had gone unto the wars,
Trusting to the mild-eyed stars,
Nightly from their azure towers,
To keep watch above the flowers,
In the midst of which all day
The red sunlight lazily lay.
Now each visitor shall confess
The sad valley's restlessness.
Nothing there is motionless,
Nothing save the airs that brood
Over the magic solitude.
Ah, by no wind are stirred those trees
That palpitate like the chill seas

The Valley of Unrest

Around the misty Hebrides!
Ah, by no wind those clouds are driven
That rustle through the unquiet heaven
Uneasily, from morn till even,
Over the violets there that lie
In myriad types of the human eye—
Over the lilies there that wave
And weep above a nameless grave!
They wave; from out their fragrant tops
Eternal dews come down in drops.
They weep; from off their delicate stems
Perennial tears descend in gems.

The City in the Sea

LO! Death has reared himself a throne
In a strange city lying alone
Far down within the dim west
Where the good and the bad and the worst and the best
Have gone to their eternal rest.
There shrines and palaces and towers
(Time-eaten towers that tremble not!)
Resemble nothing that is ours.
Around, by lifting winds forgot,
Resignedly beneath the sky
The melancholy waters lie.

No rays from the holy heaven come down
On the long night-time of that town;
But light from out the lurid sea
Streams up the turrets silently,
Gleams up the pinnacles far and free,
Up domes, up spires, up kingly halls,
Up fanes, up Babylon-like walls,

THE CITY IN THE SEA

"While from a proud tower in the town
Death looks gigantically down."

The City in the Sea

Up shadowy long-forgotten bowers
Of sculptured ivy and stone flowers,
Up many and many a marvellous shrine
Whose wreathèd friezes intertwine
The viol, the violet, and the vine.
Resignedly beneath the sky
The melancholy waters lie.
So blend the turrets and shadows there
That all seem pendulous in air,
While from a proud tower in the town
Death looks gigantically down.

There open fanes and gaping graves
Yawn level with the luminous waves;
But not the riches there that lie
In each idol's diamond eye,
Not the gayly-jewelled dead
Tempt the waters from their bed;
For no ripples curl, alas!
Along that wilderness of glass;
No swellings tell that winds may be
Upon some far-off happier sea;
No heavings hint that winds have been
On seas less hideously serene.

But lo, a stir is in the air!
The wave—there is a movement there!
As if the towers had thrust aside,
In slightly sinking, the dull tide;

The City in the Sea

As if their tops had feebly given
A void within the filmy heaven.
The waves have now a redder glow;
The hours are breathing faint and low;
And when, amid no earthly moans,
Down, down that town shall settle hence,
Hell, rising from a thousand thrones,
Shall do it reverence.

The Sleeper

T midnight, in the month of June.
　　I stand beneath the mystic moon.
　　An opiate vapor, dewy, dim,
Exhales from out her golden rim,
And, softly dripping, drop by drop,
Upon the quiet mountain top,
Steals drowsily and musically
Into the universal valley.
The rosemary nods upon the grave;
The lily lolls upon the wave;
Wrapping the fog about its breast,
The ruin moulders into rest;
Looking like Lethe, see! the lake
A conscious slumber seems to take,
And would not, for the world, awake.
All beauty sleeps! and lo! where lies
(Her casement open to the skies)
Irene, with her destinies!

The Sleeper

Oh, lady bright! can it be right—
This window open to the night ?
The wanton airs, from the tree-top,
Laughingly through the lattice drop;
The bodiless airs, a wizard rout,
Flit through thy chamber in and out,
And wave the curtain canopy
So fitfully, so fearfully,
Above the closed and fringèd lid
'Neath which thy slumb'ring soul lies hid,
That, o'er the floor and down the wall,
Like ghosts the shadows rise and fall!
Oh, lady dear, hast thou no fear ?
Why and what art thou dreaming here ?
Sure thou art come o'er far-off seas,
A wonder to these garden trees!
Strange is thy pallor! strange thy dress!
Strange, above all, thy length of tress,
And this all-solemn silentness!

The lady sleeps!   Oh, may her sleep,
Which is enduring, so be deep!
Heaven have her in its sacred keep!
This chamber changed for one more holy,
This bed for one more melancholy,
I pray to God that she may lie
Forever with unopened eye,
While the dim sheeted ghosts go by!

The Sleeper

My love, she sleeps!   Oh, may her sleep,
As it is lasting, so be deep!
Soft may the worms about her creep!
Far in the forest, dim and old,
For her may some tall vault unfold—
Some vault that oft hath flung its black
And wingèd panels fluttering back,
Triumphant, o'er the crested palls,
Of her grand family funerals;
Some sepulchre, remote, alone,
Against whose portal she hath thrown,
In childhood, many an idle stone;
Some tomb from out whose sounding door
She ne'er shall force an echo more,
Thrilling to think, poor child of sin!
It was the dead who groaned within.

Israfel[1]

IN heaven a spirit doth dwell
    " Whose heart-strings are a lute " ;
   None sing so wildly well
As the angel Israfel,
And the giddy stars (so legends tell)
Ceasing their hymns, attend the spell
  Of his voice, all mute.

Tottering above
  In her highest noon,
  The enamored moon
Blushes with love,
  While, to listen, the red levin
  (With the rapid Pleiads, even,
  Which were seven)
  Pauses in heaven.

And they say (the starry choir
  And the other listening things)

---

[1] And the angel Israfel, whose heart-strings are a lute, and who has the
sweetest voice of all God's creatures.—*Koran.*

Israfel

That Israfeli's fire
Is owing to that lyre
  By which he sits and sings—
The trembling living wire
  Of those unusual strings.

But the skies that angel trod,
  Where deep thoughts are a duty,
Where Love 's a grown-up God,
Where the Houri glances are
  Imbued with all the beauty
Which we worship in a star.

Therefore thou art not wrong,
  Israfeli, who despisest
An unimpassioned song;
To thee the laurels belong,
  Best bard, because the wisest!
Merrily live, and long!

The ecstasies above
  With thy burning measures suit;
Thy grief, thy joy, thy hate, thy love.
  With the fervor of thy lute;
  Well may the stars be mute!

Yes, heaven is thine; but this
  Is a world of sweets and sours;

Israfel

Our flowers are merely flowers,
And the shadow of thy perfect bliss
   Is the sunshine of ours.

If I could dwell
Where Israfel
   Hath dwelt, and he where I,
He might not sing so wildly well
   A mortal melody,
While a bolder note than this might swell
   From my lyre within the sky.

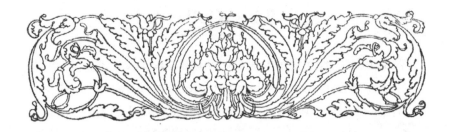

The Coliseum

TYPE of the antique Rome!   Rich reliquary
    Of lofty contemplation left to time
    By buried centuries of pomp and power!
At length, at length, after so many days
Of weary pilgrimage and burning thirst
(Thirst for the springs of lore that in thee lie),
I kneel, an altered and an humble man,
Amid thy shadows, and so drink within
My very soul thy grandeur, gloom, and glory!

Vastness, and age, and memories of eld,
Silence, and desolation, and dim night,
I feel ye now, I feel ye in your strength;
O spells more sure than e'er Judæan king
Taught in the gardens of Gethsemane!
O charms more potent than the rapt Chaldee
Ever drew down from out the quiet stars!

Here, where a hero fell, a column falls!
Here, where a mimic eagle glared in gold,
A midnight vigil holds the swarthy bat!
Here, where the dames of Rome their gilded hair

The Coliseum

Waved to the wind, now wave the reed and thistle!
Here, where on golden throne the monarch lolled,
Glides, spectre-like, unto his marble home,
Lit by the wan light of the hornèd moon,
The swift and silent lizard of the stones!
But stay! these walls, these ivy-clad arcades,
These mouldering plinths, these sad and blackened
    shafts,
These vague entablatures, this crumbling frieze,
These shattered cornices, this wreck, this ruin,
These stones—alas! these gray stones—are they all,
All of the famed and the colossal left
By the corrosive hours to fate and me ?

" Not all," the echoes answer me, " not all!
Prophetic sounds and loud arise forever
From us, and from all ruin, unto the wise,
As melody from Memnon to the sun.
We rule the hearts of mightiest men; we rule
With a despotic sway all giant minds.
We are not impotent, we pallid stones.
Not all our power is gone, not all our fame,
Not all the magic of our high renown,
Not all the wonder that encircles us,
Not all the mysteries that in us lie,
Not all the memories that hang upon
And cling around about us as a garment,
Clothing us in a robe of more than glory."

TO ONE IN PARADISE

" For alas ! alas ! with me
The light of Life is o'er !"

To One in Paradise

THOU wast that all to me, love,
　　For which my soul did pine—
　A green isle in the sea, love,
　A fountain and a shrine,
All wreathed with fairy fruits and flowers,
　And all the flowers were mine.

Ah, dream too bright to last!
　Ah, starry hope, that didst arise
But to be overcast!
　A voice from out the future cries,
" On! on! " but o'er the past
　(Dim gulf!) my spirit hovering lies
Mute, motionless, aghast!

For, alas! alas! with me
　The light of life is o'er!
　" No more—no more—no more— "
(Such language holds the solemn sea

To One in Paradise

To the sands upon the shore)
Shall bloom the thunder-blasted tree,
  Or the stricken eagle soar!

And all my days are trances,
  And all my nightly dreams
Are where thy dark eye glances,
  And where thy footstep gleams,
In what ethereal dances,
  By what eternal streams.

Hymn

T morn, at noon, at twilight dim,
    Maria! thou hast heard my hymn!
    In joy and woe, in good and ill,
Mother of God, be with me still!
When the hours flew brightly by,
And not a cloud obscured the sky,
My soul, lest it should truant be,
Thy grace did guide to thine and thee;
Now, when storms of fate o'ercast
Darkly my present and my past,
Let my future radiant shine
With sweet hopes of thee and thine!

To F——

BELOVED! amid the earnest woes
  That crowd around my earthly path
 (Drear path, alas! where grows
Not even one lonely rose)
 My soul at least a solace hath
In dreams of thee, and therein knows
An Eden of bland repose.

And thus thy memory is to me
 Like some enchanted far-off isle
In some tumultuous sea,
Some ocean throbbing far and free
 With storms, but where meanwhile
Serenest skies continually
 Just o'er that one bright island smile.

To F——S S. O——D

THOU wouldst be loved ? then let thy heart
From its present pathway part not!
Being everything which now thou art,
Be nothing which thou art not.
So with the world thy gentle ways,
Thy grace, thy more than beauty,
Shall be an endless theme of praise
And love a simple duty.

Scenes from "Politian"

AN UNPUBLISHED DRAMA

I

ROME.   A Hall in a Palace.   Alessandra and Castiglione.

Alessandra.   Thou art sad, Castiglione.

Castiglione.   Sad ? not I.
Oh, I 'm the happiest, happiest man in Rome!
A few days more, thou knowest, my Alessandra,
Will make thee mine.   Oh, I am very happy!

    Aless.   Methinks thou hast a singular way of show-
        ing
Thy happiness! what ails thee, cousin of mine ?
Why didst thou sigh so deeply ?

    Cas.   Did I sigh ?
I was not conscious of it.   It is a fashion,
A silly, a most silly fashion I have
When I am very happy.   Did I sigh ?   (*sighing*)

Scenes from "Politian"

Aless. Thou didst. Thou art not well. Thou hast
  indulged
Too much of late, and I am vexed to see it.
Late hours and wine, Castiglione, these
Will ruin thee! thou art already altered;
Thy looks are haggard; nothing so wears away
The constitution as late hours and wine.

Cas. (*musing*) Nothing, fair cousin, nothing, not
  even deep sorrow,
Wears it away like evil hours and wine;
I will amend.

Aless. Do it! I would have thee drop
Thy riotous company, too—fellows low born
Ill suit the like with old Di Broglio's heir
And Alessandra's husband.

Cas. I will drop them.

Aless. Thou wilt—thou must. Attend thou also
  more
To thy dress and equipage; they are overplain
For thy lofty rank and fashion; much depends
Upon appearances.

Cas. I 'll see to it.

Aless. Then see to it! pay more attention, sir,
To a becoming carriage; much thou wantest
In dignity.

Cas. Much, much, oh, much I want
In proper dignity.

Scenes from "Politian"

Aless. (*haughtily*) Thou mockest me, sir!

Cas. (*abstractedly*) Sweet, gentle Lalage!

Aless. Heard I aright?
I speak to him—he speaks of Lalage!
Sir Count! (*places her hand on his shoulder*) What
      art thou dreaming? he 's not well!
What ails thee, sir?

Cas. (*starting*) Cousin! fair cousin! madam!
I crave thy pardon—indeed I am not well;
Your hand from off my shoulder, if you please.
This air is most oppressive! Madam—the Duke!

Enter Di Broglio

Di Broglio. My son, I 've news for thee!—hey,
      what 's the matter? (*observing Alessandra*)
I' the pouts? Kiss her, Castiglione! kiss her,
You dog! and make it up, I say, this minute!
I 've news for you both. Politian is expected
Hourly in Rome; Politian, Earl of Leicester!
We 'll have him at the wedding. 'T is his first visit
To the imperial city.

Aless. What! Politian
Of Britain, Earl of Leicester?

Di Brog. The same, my love.
We 'll have him at the wedding. A man quite young
In years, but gray in fame. I have not seen him,
But Rumor speaks of him as of a prodigy

Scenes from " Politian "

Pre-eminent in arts, and arms, and wealth,
And high descent.   We 'll have him at the wedding.
   Aless.   I have heard much of this Politian.
Gay, volatile, and giddy, is he not ?
And little given to thinking.
   Di Brog.   Far from it, love.
No branch, they say, of all philosophy
So deep abstruse he has not mastered it.
Learned as few are learned.
   Aless.   'T is very strange!
I have known men have seen Politian
And sought his company.   They speak of him
As of one who entered madly into life,
Drinking the cup of pleasure to the dregs.
   Cas.   Ridiculous!   Now I have seen Politian
And know him well; nor learned nor mirthful he.
He is a dreamer and a man shut out
From common passions.
   Di Brog.   Children, we disagree.
Let us go forth and taste the fragrant air
Of the garden.   Did I dream, or did I hear
Politian was a melancholy man ?   *(exeunt)*

Scenes from "Politian"

II

ROME. A Lady's apartment, with a window open and looking into a garden. Lalage, in deep mourning, reading at a table on which lie some books and a hand mirror. In the background Jacinta (a servant maid) leans carelessly upon a chair.

Lalage. Jacinta! is it thou?

Jacinta. (*pertly*) Yes, ma'am, I 'm here.

Lal. I did not know, Jacinta, you were in waiting.
Sit down! let not my presence trouble you;
Sit down! for I am humble, most humble.

Jac. (*aside*) 'T is time.

    (*Jacinta seats herself in a sidelong manner upon
        the chair, resting her elbows upon the back,
        and regarding her mistress with a contemp-
        tuous look. Lalage continues to read*)

Lal. " It in another climate," so he said,
Bore a bright golden flower, but not i' this soil! "

    (*pauses—turns over some leaves, and resumes*)
" No lingering winters there, nor snow, nor shower,
But Ocean ever, to refresh mankind,
Breathes the shrill spirit of the western wind."
Oh, beautiful! most beautiful! how like
To what my fevered soul doth dream of heaven!
O happy land! (*pauses*) She died! the maiden died!
O still more happy maiden who couldst die!
Jacinta!

    (*Jacinta returns no answer, and Lalage pres-
        ently resumes.*)

Scenes from " Politian "

Again! a similar tale
Told of a beauteous dame beyond the sea!
Thus speaketh one Ferdinand in the words of the play:
" She died full young "; one Bossola answers him:
" I think not so—her infelicity
Seemed to have years too many."—Ah, luckless lady!
Jacinta! (*still no answer*)
        Here 's a far sterner story,
But like—oh, very like in its despair—
Of that Egyptian queen, winning so easily
A thousand hearts; losing at length her own.
She died.   Thus endeth the history; and her maids
Lean over her and weep—two gentle maids
With gentle names, Eiros and Charmion!
Rainbow and Dove!   Jacinta!

  Jac. (*pettishly*)   Madam, what is it ?

  Lal.   Wilt thou, my good Jacinta, be so kind
As go down in the library and bring me
The Holy Evangelists.

  Jac.   Pshaw!   (*exit*)

  Lal.   If there be balm
For the wounded spirit in Gilead it is there!
Dew in the night-time of my bitter trouble
Will there be found—" dew sweeter far than that
Which hangs like chains of pearl on Hermon Hill."

      (*Re-enter Jacinta, and throws a volume on the
        table.*)

Scenes from " Politian "

There, ma'am, 's the book.   Indeed she is very trouble-
 some.   (*aside*)
 Lal. (*astonished*) What didst thou say, Jacinta ?
 Have I done aught
To grieve thee or to vex thee ? I am sorry.
For thou hast served me long and ever been
Trustworthy and respectful. (***resumes her reading***)
 Jac. I can't believe
She has any more jewels; no, no, she gave me all.
             (*aside*)

 Lal. What didst thou say, Jacinta ? Now I be-
 think me
Thou hast not spoken lately of thy wedding.
How fares good Ugo ? and when is it to be ?
Can I do aught ? is there no further aid
Thou needest, Jacinta ?
 Jac. Is there no further aid!
That 's meant for me. (*aside*) I 'm sure, madam,
 you need not
Be always throwing those jewels in my teeth.
 Lal. Jewels ? Jacinta,—now indeed, Jacinta,
I thought not of the jewels.
 Jac. Oh, perhaps not;
But then I might have sworn it. After all,
There 's Ugo says the ring is only paste,
For he 's sure the Count Castiglione never
Would have given a real diamond to such as you;

SCENES FROM "POLITIAN"

"Fair mirror and true, now tell me (for thou canst)
A tale, a pretty tale and heed thou not
Though it be rife with woe."

Scenes from " Politian "

And at the best I 'm certain, madam, you cannot
Have use for jewels now.   But I might have sworn it.

(exit)

(Lalage bursts into tears and leans her head
upon the table; after a short pause raises it.)

Lal.   Poor Lalage! and is it come to this ?
Thy servant maid! but courage! 't is but a viper
Whom thou hast cherished to sting thee to the soul!

(taking up the mirror)

Ha! here at least 's a friend—too much a friend
In earlier days; a friend will not deceive thee.
Fair mirror and true, now tell me (for thou canst)
A tale, a pretty tale, and heed thou not
Though it be rife with woe.   It answers me.
It speaks of sunken eyes, and wasted cheeks,
And Beauty long deceased—remembers me
Of Joy departed; Hope, the Seraph Hope,
Inurned and entombed; now, in a tone
Low, sad, and solemn, but most audible,
Whispers of early grave untimely yawning
For ruined maid.   Fair mirror and true, thou liest not!
Thou hast no end to gain, no heart to break;
Castiglione lied who said he loved—
Thou true, he false! false! false!

(While she speaks, a monk enters her apart-
ment, and approaches unobserved.)

Monk.   Refuge thou hast,
Sweet daughter, in heaven.   Think of eternal things;

Scenes from "Politian"

Give up thy soul to penitence, and pray!
   Lal. (*arising hurriedly*) I cannot pray! My soul
      is at war with God!
The frightful sounds of merriment below
Disturb my senses; go! I cannot pray;
The sweet airs from the garden worry me;
Thy presence grieves me: go! thy priestly raiment
Fills me with dread; thy ebony crucifix
With horror and awe!
   Monk. Think of thy precious soul!
   Lal. Think of my early days! think of my father
And mother in heaven; think of our quiet home,
And the rivulet that ran before the door;
Think of my little sisters; think of them!
And think of me!—think of my trusting love
And confidence—his vows—my ruin—think, think
Of my unspeakable misery! begone!
Yet stay, yet stay, what was it thou saidst of prayer
And penitence? Didst thou not speak of faith
And vows before the throne?
   Monk. I did.
   Lal. 'T is well.
There is a vow were fitting should be made—
A sacred vow, imperative and urgent,
A solemn vow!
   Monk. Daughter, this zeal is well!
   Lal. Father, this zeal is any thing but well!
Hast thou a crucifix fit for this thing!

Scenes from "Politian"

A crucifix whereon to register
This sacred vow ?   (*he hands her his own*)
Not that—oh, no! no! no!   (*shuddering*)
Not that, not that!   I tell thee, holy man,
Thy raiments and thy ebony cross affright **me**!
Stand back!   I have a crucifix myself,
I have a crucifix!   Methinks 't were fitting
The deed, the vow, the symbol of the deed,
And the deed's register should tally, father!
　　　(*draws a cross-handled dagger and raises it on
　　　　high*)
Behold the cross wherewith a vow like mine
Is written in heaven!
　　Monk.   Thy words are madness, daughter,
And speak a purpose unholy; thy lips are livid,
Thine eyes are wild; tempt not the wrath divine!
Pause ere too late! oh, be not, be not rash!
Swear not the oath, oh, swear it not!
　　Lal.   'T is sworn!

III

An Apartment in a Palace.   Politian and Baldazzar.

Baldazzar.   Arouse thee now, Politian!
Thou must not—nay, indeed, indeed, thou shalt **not**
Give way unto these humors.   Be thyself!
Shake off the idle fancies that beset **thee**,
And live, for now thou diest!
　　Politian.   Not so, Baldazzar!
Surely I live.

Scenes from "Politian"

Bal.   Politian, it doth grieve me
To see thee thus.

 Pol.   Baldazzar, it doth grieve me
To give thee cause for grief, my honored friend.
Command me, sir! what wouldst thou have me do ?
At thy behest I will shake off that nature
Which from my forefathers I did inherit,
Which with my mother's milk I did imbibe,
And be no more Politian, but some other.
Command me, sir!

 Bal.   To the field then; to the field;
To the senate or the field.

 Pol.   Alas! alas!
There is an imp would follow me even there!
There is an imp hath followed me even there!
There is——what voice was that ?

 Bal.   I heard it not.
I heard not any voice except thine own,
And the echo of thine own.

 Pol.   Then I but dreamed.

 Bal.   Give not thy soul to dreams: the camp, the
  court
Befit thee; Fame awaits thee—Glory calls—
And her the trumpet-tongued thou wilt not hear
In hearkening to imaginary sounds
And phantom voices.

 Pol.   It is a phantom voice!
Didst thou not hear it then ?

Scenes from "Politian"

Bal. I heard it not.

Pol. Thou heardst it not? Baldazzar, speak no
    more

To me, Politian, of thy camps and courts.

Oh! I am sick, sick, sick, even unto death,

Of the hollow and high-sounding vanities

Of the populous earth! Bear with me yet a while!

We have been boys together; school-fellows;

And now are friends, yet shall not be so long;

For in the eternal city thou shalt do me

A kind and gentle office, and a Power—

A Power august, benignant, and supreme—

Shall then absolve thee of all further duties

Unto thy friend.

Bal. Thou speakest a fearful riddle

I will not understand.

Pol. Yet now as fate

Approaches, and the hours are breathing low,

The sands of time are changed to golden grains,

And dazzle me, Baldazzar. Alas! alas!

I cannot die, having within my heart

So keen a relish for the beautiful

As has been kindled within it. Methinks the air

Is balmier now than it was wont to be;

Rich melodies are floating in the winds,

A rarer loveliness bedecks the earth,

And with a holier lustre the quiet moon

Sitteth in heaven.—Hist! hist! thou canst not say

Scenes from "Politian"

Thou hearest not now, Baldazzar?

    Bal.   Indeed I hear not.

    Pol.   Not hear it! listen now, listen! the faintest
       sound
And yet the sweetest that ear ever heard!
A lady's voice, and sorrow in the tone!
Baldazzar, it oppresses me like a spell!
Again! again! how solemnly it falls
Into my heart of hearts! that eloquent voice
Surely I never heard; yet it were well
Had I but heard it with its thrilling tones
In earlier days!

    Bal.   I myself hear it now.
Be still! the voice, if I mistake not greatly,
Proceeds from yonder lattice which you may see
Very plainly through the window; it belongs,
Does it not? unto this palace of the Duke.
The singer is undoubtedly beneath
The roof of his Excellency; and perhaps
Is even that Alessandra of whom he spoke
As the betrothed of Castiglione,
His son and heir.

    Pol.   Be still! it comes again!

     Voice (*very faintly*)

            " And is thy heart so strong
              As for to leave me thus
            Who hath loved thee so long
            In wealth and woe among?

Scenes from " Politian "

> *And is thy heart so strong*
> *As for to leave me thus?*
> > *Say nay—say nay!* "

Bal.   The song is English, and I oft have heard it
In merry England—never so plaintively.
Hist! hist! it comes again!

> *Voice* (*more loudly*)
> > *" Is it so strong*
> > *As for to leave me thus*
> > *Who hath loved thee so long,*
> > *In wealth and woe among?*
> > *And is thy heart so strong*
> > *As for to leave me thus?*
> > > *Say nay—say nay!* '

Bal.   'T is hushed and all is still!

Pol.   All is not still.

Bal.   Let us go down.

Pol.   Go down, Baldazzar, go!

Bal.   The hour is growing late; the Duke awaits
        us;
Thy presence is expected in the hall
Below.   What ails thee, Earl Politian ?

> *Voice* (*distinctly*)
> > *" Who hath loved thee so long,*
> > *In wealth and woe among,*
> > *And is thy heart so strong?*
> > > *Say nay—say nay!* "

Bal.   Let us descend; 't is time.   Politian, give

Scenes from "Politian"

These fancies to the wind.   Remember, pray,
Your bearing lately savored much of rudeness
Unto the Duke.   Arouse thee, and remember!
  Pol.   Remember? I do. Lead on! I do remem-
       ber.   (*going*)
Let us descend.   Believe me, I would give,
Freely would give, the broad lands of my earldom
To look upon the face hidden by yon lattice—
" To gaze upon that veiled face, and hear
Once more that silent tongue."
  Bal.   Let me beg you, sir,
Descend with me; the Duke may be offended.
Let us go down, I pray you.
  (*Voice loudly*)   *Say nay! — say nay!*
  Pol. (*aside*)   'T is strange, 't is very strange; me-
      thought the voice
Chimed in with my desires and bade me stay!
               (*approaching the window*)
Sweet voice! I heed thee, and will surely stay.
Now be this fancy, by heaven, or be it fate,
Still will I not descend.   Baldazzar, make
Apology unto the Duke for me;
I go not down to-night.
  Bal.   Your lordship's pleasure
Shall be attended to.   Good night, Politian.
  Pol.   Good night, my friend, good night.

Scenes from "Politian"

IV

Lalage. And dost thou speak of love
To me, Politian ? dost thou speak of love
To Lalage ? ah, woe! ah, woe is me!
This mockery is most cruel, most cruel indeed!
  Politian. Weep not! oh, sob not thus! thy **bitter**
    tears
Will madden me.   Oh, mourn not, Lalage;
Be comforted!   I know, I know it all,
And still I speak of love.   Look at me, **brightest**
And beautiful Lalage! turn here thine eyes!
Thou askest me if I could speak of love,
Knowing what I know, and seeing what I have seen.
Thou askest me that, and thus I answer thee,
Thus on my bended knee I answer thee.   (*kneeling*)
Sweet Lalage, I love thee, love thee, love thee!
Thro' good and ill, thro' weal and woe I love thee!
Not mother, with her first-born on her knee,
Thrills with intenser love than I for thee.
Not on God's altar, in any time or clime,
Burned there a holier fire than burneth now
Within my spirit for thee.   And do I love ? (*arising*)
Even for thy woes I love thee, even for thy woes,
Thy beauty and thy woes.
  Lal. Alas, proud Earl,
Thou dost forget thyself, remembering me!

Scenes from "Politian"

How, in thy father's halls, among the maidens
Pure and reproachless of thy princely line,
Could the dishonored Lalage abide?
Thy wife, and with a tainted memory—
My seared and blighted name, how would it tally
With the ancestral honors of thy house,
And with thy glory?

   Pol. Speak not to me of glory!
I hate, I loathe the name! I do abhor
The unsatisfactory and ideal thing.
Art thou not Lalage and I Politian?
Do I not love? art thou not beautiful?
What need we more? Ha! glory! now speak not of
       it.
By all I hold most sacred and most solemn;
By all my wishes now, my fears hereafter;
By all I scorn on earth and hope in heaven,
There is no deed I would more glory in
Than in thy cause to scoff at this same glory
And trample it under foot. What matters it,
What matters it, my fairest and my best,
That we go down unhonored and forgotten
Into the dust, so we descend together?
Descend together, and then—and then perchance—

   Lal. Why dost thou pause, Politian?

   Pol. And then perchance
Arise together, Lalage, and roam
The starry and quiet dwellings of the blest,

Scenes from "Politian"

And still—

    Lal. Why dost thou pause, Politian?

    Pol. And still together—together.

    Lal. Now, Earl of Leicester!

Thou lovest me, and in my heart of hearts

I feel thou lovest me truly.

    Pol. Oh, Lalage! (*throwing himself upon his knee*)

And lovest thou me?

    Lal. Hist! hush! within the gloom

Of yonder trees methought a figure passed—

A spectral figure, solemn, and slow, and noiseless—

Like the grim shadow Conscience, solemn and noise-

        less.   (*walks across and returns*)

I was mistaken; 't was but a giant bough

Stirred by the autumn wind. Politian!

    Pol. My Lalage, my love! why art thou moved?

Why dost thou turn so pale? Not Conscience' self,

Far less a shadow which thou likenest to it,

Should shake the firm spirit thus. But the night wind

Is chilly, and these melancholy boughs

Throw over all things a gloom.

    Lal. Politian,

Thou speakest to me of love. Knowest thou the land

With which all tongues are busy—a land new found,

Miraculously found by one of Genoa,

A thousand leagues within the golden west?

A fairy land of flowers, and fruit, and sunshine,

And crystal lakes, and overarching forests,

Scenes from "Politian"

And mountains, around whose towering summits the
    winds
Of heaven untrammelled flow, which air to breathe
Is happiness now, and will be freedom hereafter
In days that are to come ?

   Pol. Oh, wilt thou, wilt thou
Fly to that paradise ? my Lalage, wilt thou
Fly thither with me ? There care shall be forgotten,
And sorrow shall be no more, and Eros be all.
And life shall then be mine, for I will live
For thee, and in thine eyes, and thou shalt be
No more a mourner; but the radiant Joys
Shall wait upon thee, and the angel Hope
Attend thee ever; and I will kneel to thee,
And worship thee, and call thee my beloved,
My all; oh, wilt thou, wilt thou, Lalage,
Fly thither with me ?

   Lal. A deed is to be done—
Castiglione lives !

   Pol. And he shall die.   *(exit)*

   Lal. (*after a pause*) And — he — shall — die ? —
    alas !
Castiglione die ? Who spoke the words ?
Where am I ? what was it he said ? Politian !
Thou art not gone—thou art not gone, Politian !
I feel thou art not gone, yet dare not look
Lest I behold thee not; thou couldst not go
With those words upon thy lips—oh, speak to me !

Scenes from " Politian "

And let me hear thy voice—one word, one word,
To say thou art not gone; one little sentence,
To say how thou dost scorn, how thou dost hate
My womanly weakness! Ha! ha! thou art not
      gone—
Oh, speak to me! I knew thou wouldst not go!
I knew thou wouldst not, couldst not, durst not go.
Villain, thou art not gone—thou mockest me!
And thus I clutch thee, thus! He is gone, he is gone—
Gone—gone. Where am I ? 't is well, 't is very well;
So that the blade be keen, the blow be sure,
'T is well, 't is very well—alas! alas!

V

The Suburbs. Politian alone.

Politian. This weakness grows upon me. I am
      faint,
And much I fear me ill; it will not do
To die ere I have lived! Stay, stay thy hand,
O Azrael, yet awhile! Prince of the powers
Of darkness and the tomb, oh, pity me!
Oh, pity me! let me not perish now,
In the budding of my paradisal hope!
Give me to live yet, yet a little while:
'T is I who pray for life; I who so late
Demanded but to die! What sayeth the Count ?
        Enter Baldazzar.

Scenes from " Politian "

Baldazzar.   That, knowing no cause of quarrel or
    of feud
Between the Earl Politian and himself,
He doth decline your cartel.

   Pol.   What didst thou say ?
What answer was it you brought me, good Baldazzar ?
With what excessive fragrance the zephyr comes
Laden from yonder bowers ! a fairer day,
Or one more worthy Italy, methinks
No mortal eyes have seen !—what said the Count ?

   Bal.   That he, Castiglione, not being aware
Of any feud existing, or any cause
Of quarrel between your lordship and himself,
Cannot accept the challenge.

   Pol.   It is most true;
All this is very true.   When saw you, sir,
When saw you now, Baldazzar, in the frigid
Ungenial Britain which we left so lately,
A heaven so calm as this, so utterly free
From the evil taint of clouds ?—and he did say ?

   Bal.   No more, my lord, than I have told you, sir:
The Count Castiglione will not fight,
Having no cause for quarrel.

   Pol.   Now this is true,
All very true.   Thou art my friend, Baldazzar,
And I have not forgotten it; thou 'lt do me
A piece of service; wilt thou go back and sav
Unto this man, that I, the Earl of Leicester,

Scenes from " Politian "

Hold him a villain ? thus much, I prythee, say
Unto the Count; it is exceeding just
He should have cause for quarrel.

   Bal. My lord!—my friend!——

   Pol. (*aside*) 'T is he—he comes himself! (*aloud*)
      Thou reasonest well;
I know what thou wouldst say: not send the message.
Well, I will think of it; I will not send it.
Now prythee, leave me; hither doth come a person
With whom affairs of a most private nature
I would adjust.

   Bal. I go; to-morrow we meet,
Do we not ? at the Vatican.

   Pol. At the Vatican.

              Enter Castiglione.

   Cas. The Earl of Leicester here ?

   Pol. I am the Earl of Leicester, and thou seest,
Dost thou not ? that I am here.

   Cas. My lord, some strange,
Some singular mistake—misunderstanding—
Hath without doubt arisen: thou hast been urged
Thereby, in heat of anger, to address
Some words most unaccountable, in writing,
To me, Castiglione; the bearer being
Baldazzar, Duke of Surrey. I am aware
Of nothing which might warrant thee in this thing,
Having given thee no offence. Ha! am I right ?
'T was a mistake ? undoubtedly; we all

Scenes from "Politian"

Do err at times.

   Pol.   Draw, villain, and prate no more!

   Cas.   Ha! draw? and villain? have at thee then
       at once,
Proud Earl!

   Pol.   (*drawing*) Thus to the expiatory tomb,
Untimely sepulchre, I do devote thee
In the name of Lalage!

   Cas. (*letting fall his sword and recoiling to the ex-
tremity of the stage*)

                        Of Lalage!
Hold off—thy sacred hand!—avaunt, I say!
Avaunt! I will not fight thee; indeed I dare not.

   Pol.   Thou wilt not fight with me, didst say, Sir
       Count?
Shall I be baffled thus? now this is well;
Didst say thou darest not? Ha!

   Cas.   I dare not, dare not;
Hold off thy hand—with that beloved name
So fresh upon thy lips I will not fight thee.
I cannot; dare not.

   Pol.   Now by my halidom
I do believe thee! coward, I do believe thee!

   Cas.   Ha! coward! this may not be!

       (*clutches his sword and staggers towards Poli-
          tian, but his purpose is changed before reach-
          ing him, and he falls upon his knee at the
          feet of the Earl*)

Scenes from " Politian "

                                        Alas! my lord,
It is, it is most true.   In such a cause
I am the veriest coward.   Oh, pity me!

   Pol. (*greatly softened*)   Alas!   I do, indeed I pity
     thee.

   Cas.   And Lalage—

   Pol.   Scoundrel! arise and die!

   Cas.   It needeth not be; thus—thus—oh, let me die
Thus on my bended knee!   It were most fitting
That in this deep humiliation I perish;
For in the fight I will not raise a hand
Against thee, Earl of Leicester.   Strike thou home—
                              (*baring his bosom*)
Here is no let or hindrance to thy weapon—
Strike home.   I will not fight thee.

   Pol.   Now s'death and hell!
Am I not—am I not sorely, grievously tempted
To take thee at thy word ?   But mark me, sir:
Think not to fly me thus.   Do thou prepare
For public insults in the streets, before
The eyes of the citizens.   I 'll follow thee;
Like an avenging spirit I 'll follow thee
Even unto death.   Before those whom thou lovest—
Before all Rome I 'll taunt thee, villain, I 'll taunt thee,
Dost hear ? with cowardice—thou wilt not fight me ?
Thou liest! thou shalt!   (*exit*)

   Cas.   Now this indeed is just!
Most righteous, and most just, avenging Heaven!

To Zante

FAIR isle, that from the fairest of all flowers
    Thy gentlest of all gentle names dost take!
    How many memories of what radiant hours
At sight of thee and thine at once awake!
How many scenes of what departed bliss!
    How many thoughts of what entombèd hopes!
How many visions of a maiden that is
    No more—no more upon thy verdant slopes!
No more! alas, that magical sad sound
    Transforming all! Thy charms shall please no
        more!
Thy memory no more! Accursèd ground
    Henceforth I hold thy flower-enamelled shore,
O hyacinthine isle! O purple Zante!
    "Isola d' oro! Fior di Levante!"

Bridal Ballad

THE ring is on my hand,
    And the wreath is on my brow;
  Satins and jewels grand
Are all at my command,
  And I am happy now.

And my lord he loves me well;
  But when first he breathed his vow
I felt my bosom swell,
For the words rang as a knell,
And the voice seemed his who fell
In the battle down the dell,
  And who is happy now.

But he spoke to reassure me,
  And he kissed my pallid brow,
While a revery came o'er me,
And to the churchyard bore me,
And I sighed to him before me,
Thinking him dead D'Elormie,
  " Oh, I am happy now! "

Bridal Ballad

And thus the words were spoken,
　And this the plighted vow,
And though my faith be broken,
And though my heart be broken,
Behold the golden token
　That proves me happy now!

Would God I could awaken!
　For I dream I know not how,
And my soul is sorely shaken
Lest an evil step be taken,
Lest the dead who is forsaken
　May not be happy now.

The Haunted Palace

IN the greenest of our valleys
  By good angels tenanted,
    Once a fair and stately palace—
Radiant palace—reared its head.
In the monarch Thought's dominion
  It stood there!
Never seraph spread a pinion
  Over fabric half so fair!

Banners yellow, glorious, golden,
  On its roof did float and flow
(This, all this, was in the olden
  Time long ago),
And every gentle air that dallied,
  In that sweet day,
Along the ramparts plumed and pallid,
  A wingèd odor went away.

Wanderers in that happy valley
  Through two luminous windows saw

The Haunted Palace

Spirits moving musically
  To a lute's well-tunèd law,
Round about a throne where, sitting
  (Porphyrogene!)
In state his glory well befitting,
  The ruler of the realm was seen.

And all with pearl and ruby glowing
  Was the fair palace-door,
Through which came flowing, flowing, flowing,
  And sparkling evermore,
A troop of Echoes, whose sweet duty
  Was but to sing,
In voices of surpassing beauty,
  The wit and wisdom of their king.

But evil things, in robes of sorrow,
  Assailed the monarch's high estate.
(Ah, let us mourn! for never morrow
  Shall dawn upon him desolate!)
And round about his home, the glory
  That blushed and bloomed
Is but a dim-remembered story
  Of the old time entombed.

And travellers now, within that valley,
  Through the red-litten windows see
Vast forms, that move fantastically

The Haunted Palace

To a discordant melody,
While, like a ghastly rapid river,
Through the pale door
A hideous throng rush out forever
And laugh, but smile no more.

Silence

THERE are some qualities, some incorporate
        things,
        That have a double life, which thus is made
A type of that twin entity which springs
    From matter and light, evinced in solid and shade.
There is a twofold Silence—sea and shore—
    Body and soul.   One dwells in lonely places,
    Newly with grass o'ergrown; some solemn graces,
Some human memories and tearful lore,
Render him terrorless: his name 's " No More."
He is the corporate Silence: dread him not!
    No power hath he of evil in himself;
But should some urgent fate (untimely lot!)
    Bring thee to meet his shadow (nameless elf,
That haunteth the lone regions where hath trod
No foot of man), commend thyself to God!

The Conqueror Worm

LO! 't is a gala night
    Within the lonesome latter years!
    An angel throng, bewinged, bedight
  In veils, and drowned in tears,
Sit in a theatre, to see
  A play of hopes and fears,
While the orchestra breathes fitfully
  The music of the spheres.

Mimes, in the form of God on high,
  Mutter and mumble low,
And hither and thither fly;
  Mere puppets they, who come and go
At bidding of vast formless things
  That shift the scenery to and fro,
Flapping from out their condor wings
  Invisible woe!

The Conqueror Worm

That motley drama—oh, be sure
   It shall not be forgot!
With its phantom chased for evermore,
   By a crowd that seize it not,
Through a circle that ever returneth in
   To the self-same spot,
And much of madness, and more of sin,
   And horror the soul of the plot.

But see, amid the mimic rout
   A crawling shape intrude!
A blood-red thing that writhes from out
   The scenic solitude!
It writhes! it writhes! with mortal pangs
   The mimes become its food,
And the angels sob at vermin fangs
   In human gore imbued.

Out, out are the lights, out all!
   And, over each quivering form,
The curtain, a funeral pall,
   Comes down with the rush of a storm,
And the angels, all pallid and wan,
   Uprising, unveiling, affirm
That the play is the tragedy " Man,"
   And its hero the Conqueror Worm.

DREAMLAND

Dreamland

BY a route obscure and lonely,
 Haunted by ill angels only,
 Where an Eidolon, named Night,
On a black throne reigns upright,
I have reached these lands but newly
From an ultimate dim Thule—
From a wild weird clime that lieth, sublime,
 Out of Space, out of Time.

Bottomless vales and boundless floods,
And chasms and caves and Titan woods,
With forms that no man can discover
For the dews that drip all over;
Mountains toppling evermore
Into seas without a shore;
Seas that restlessly aspire,
Surging, unto skies of fire;
Lakes that endlessly outspread
Their lone waters lone and dead,

Dreamland

Their still waters—still and chilly
With the snows of the lolling lily.

By the lakes that thus outspread
Their lone waters, lone and dead,
Their sad waters, sad and chilly
With the snows of the lolling lily,
By the mountains, near the river
Murmuring lowly, murmuring ever,
By the gray woods, by the swamp
Where the toad and the newt encamp,
By the dismal tarns and pools
    Where dwell the Ghouls,
By each spot the most unholy,
In each nook most melancholy,
There the traveller meets aghast
Sheeted memories of the past—
Shrouded forms that start and sigh
As they pass the wanderer by—
White-robed forms of friends long given,
In agony, to the earth—and heaven.

For the heart whose woes are legion
'T is a peaceful, soothing region;
For the spirit that walks in shadow
'T is—oh, 't is an Eldorado!
But the traveller, travelling through it,
May not, dare not openly view it;

Dreamland

Never its mysteries are exposed
To the weak human eye unclosed;
So wills its king, who hath forbid
The uplifting of the fringed lid;
And thus the sad soul that here passes
Beholds it but through darkened glasses.

By a route obscure and lonely,
Haunted by ill angels only,
Where an Eidolon, named Night,
On a black throne reigns upright,
I have wandered home but newly
From this ultimate dim Thule.

The Raven

ONCE upon a midnight dreary, while I pondered, weak and weary,
    Over many a quaint and curious volume of forgotten lore,
While I nodded, nearly napping, suddenly there came a tapping,
As of some one gently rapping, rapping at my chamber door.
" 'T is some visitor," I muttered, " tapping at my chamber door,
        Only this and nothing more."

Ah, distinctly I remember it was in the bleak December,
And each separate dying ember wrought its ghost upon the floor.

The Raven

Eagerly I wished the morrow; vainly I had sought to
borrow
From my books surcease of sorrow—sorrow for the
lost Lenore,
For the rare and radiant maiden whom the angels
name Lenore,
Nameless here for evermore.

And the silken sad uncertain rustling of each purple
curtain
Thrilled me, filled me with fantastic terrors never
felt before;
So that now, to still the beating of my heart, I stood
repeating:
" 'T is some visitor entreating entrance at my cham-
ber door—
Some late visitor entreating entrance at my chamber
door;
This it is and nothing more."

Presently my soul grew stronger; hesitating then no
longer,
" Sir," said I, " or Madam, truly your forgiveness I
implore;
But the fact is I was napping, and so gently you came
rapping,
And so faintly you came tapping, tapping at my cham-
ber door,

The Raven

That I scarce was sure I heard you "—here I opened
    wide the door;
                Darkness there and nothing more.

Deep into that darkness peering, long I stood there
    wondering, fearing,
Doubting, dreaming dreams no mortals ever dared to
    dream before;
But the silence was unbroken, and the stillness gave
    no token,
And the only word there spoken was the whispered
    word, " Lenore! "
This I whispered, and an echo murmured back the
    word, " Lenore! "
                Merely this and nothing more.

Back into the chamber turning, all my soul within me
    burning,
Soon again I heard a tapping something louder than
    before.
" Surely," said I, " surely that is something at my
    window lattice;
Let me see, then, what thereat is, and this mystery
    explore;
Let my heart be still a moment, and this mystery
    explore;
                'T is the wind and nothing more."

The Raven

Open here I flung the shutter, when, with many a flirt
and flutter,
In there stepped a stately Raven of the saintly days of
yore.
Not the least obeisance made he; not a minute stopped
or stayed ne,
But, with mien of lord or lady, perched above my
chamber door,
Perched upon a bust of Pallas just above my chamber
door,
   Perched, and sat, and nothing more.

Then this ebony bird beguiling my sad fancy into
smiling,
By the grave and stern decorum of the countenance
it wore,
" Though thy crest be shorn and shaven, thou," I said,
" art sure no craven,
Ghastly grim and ancient Raven wandering from the
Nightly shore;
Tell me what thy lordly name is on the Night's Plu-
tonian shore! "
   Quoth the Raven, " Nevermore."

Much I marvelled this ungainly fowl to hear discourse
so plainly,
Though its answer little meaning, little relevancy
bore;

The Raven

For we cannot help agreeing that no living human
    being
Ever yet was blessed with seeing bird above his cham-
    ber door—
Bird or beast upon the sculptured bust above his
    chamber door,
                  With such name as " Nevermore."

But the Raven, sitting lonely on that placid bust, spoke
    only
That one word, as if his soul in that one word he did
    outpour.
Nothing further then he uttered; not a feather then
    he fluttered;
Till I scarcely more than muttered: " Other friends
    have flown before;
On the morrow *he* will leave me as my hopes have
    flown before."
                  Then the bird said, " Nevermore."

Startled at the stillness broken by reply so aptly
    spoken,
" Doubtless," said I, " what it utters is its only stock
    and store,
Caught from some unhappy master whom unmerciful
    disaster
Followed fast and followed faster till his songs one
    burden bore,

The Raven

Till the dirges of his hope that melancholy burden
bore

      Of ' Never—nevermore.' "

But the Raven still beguiling all my sad soul into
  smiling,
Straight I wheeled a cushioned seat in front of bird
  and bust and door;
Then, upon the velvet sinking, I betook myself to
  linking
Fancy unto fancy, thinking what this ominous bird
  of yore,
What this grim, ungainly, ghastly, gaunt, and omi-
  nous bird of yore

      Meant in croaking " Nevermore."

This I sat engaged in guessing, but no syllable ex-
  pressing
To the fowl whose fiery eyes now burned into my
  bosom's core;
This and more I sat divining, with my head at ease
  reclining
On the cushion's velvet lining that the lamp-light
  gloated o'er,
But whose velvet violet lining with the lamp-light
  gloating o'er

      She shall press, ah, nevermore!

The Raven

Then, methought, the air grew denser, perfumed from
    an unseen censer
Swung by seraphim whose foot-falls tinkled on the
    tufted floor.
" Wretch," I cried, " thy God hath lent thee—by
    these angels he hath sent thee
Respite, respite and nepenthe from thy memories of
    Lenore!
Quaff, oh quaff this kind nepenthe and forget this lost
    Lenore! "
                Quoth the Raven, " Nevermore."

" Prophet! " said I, " thing of evil! prophet still, if
    bird or devil!
Whether Tempter sent or whether tempest tossed thee
    here ashore,
Desolate, yet all undaunted, on this desert land en-
    chanted,
On this home by Horror haunted, tell me truly, I
    implore,
Is there, is there balm in Gilead ? tell me, tell me, I
    implore! "
                Quoth the Raven, " Nevermore."

" Prophet! " said I, " thing of evil! prophet still, if
    bird or devil!
By that heaven that bends above us, by that God we
    both adore,

The Raven

Tell this soul with sorrow laden if, within the distant
    Aidenn,
It shall clasp a sainted maiden whom the angels name
    Lenore,
Clasp a rare and radiant maiden whom the angels
    name Lenore."
               Quoth the Raven, " Nevermore."

" Be that word our sign of parting, bird or fiend!" I
    shrieked, upstarting;
" Get thee back into the tempest and the night's Plu-
    tonian shore!
Leave no black plume as a token of that lie thy soul
    hath spoken!
Leave my loneliness unbroken! quit the bust above
    my door!
Take thy beak from out my heart, and take thy form
    from off my door!"
               Quoth the Raven, " Nevermore."

And the Raven, never flitting, still is sitting, still is
    sitting
On the pallid bust of Pallas just above my chamber
    door;
And his eyes have all the seeming of a demon's that
    is dreaming,

The Raven

And the lamp-light o'er him streaming throws his
    shadow on the floor;
And my soul from out that shadow that lies floating
    on the floor

              Shall be lifted—nevermore!

Eulalie

I DWELT alone
    In a world of moan,
       And my soul was a stagnant tide,
Till the fair and gentle Eulalie became my blushing
    bride—
Till the yellow-haired young Eulalie became my
    smiling bride.

        Ah, less—less bright
        The stars of night
      Than the eyes of the radiaut girl!
        And never a flake
        That the vapor can make
      With the moon-tints of purple and pearl
Can vie with the modest Eulalie's most unregarded
    curl,
Can compare with the bright-eyed Eulalie's most
    humble and careless curl.

Eulalie

Now doubt, now pain
Come never again,
For her soul gives me sigh for sigh,
And all day long
Shines, bright and strong,
Astarté within the sky,
While ever to her dear Eulalie upturns her matron
eye,
While ever to her young Eulalie upturns her violet eye。

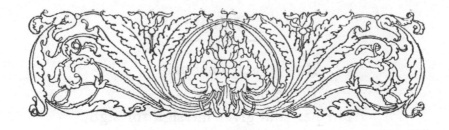

To M. L. S.

OF all who hail thy presence as the morning,
　　Of all to whom thine absence is the night—
　　The blotting utterly from out high heaven
The sacred sun—of all who, weeping, bless thee
Hourly for hope, for life, ah! above all,
For the resurrection of deep-buried faith
In truth, in virtue, in humanity;
Of all who, on despair's unhallowed bed
Lying down to die, have suddenly arisen
At thy soft-murmured words, " Let there be light! "
At the soft-murmured words that were fulfilled
In the seraphic glancing of thine eyes;
Of all who owe thee most, whose gratitude
Nearest resembles worship, oh, remember
The truest, the most fervently devoted,
And think that these weak lines are written by him,—
By him who, as he pens them, thrills to think
His spirit is communing with an angel's.

Ulalume

THE skies they were ashen and sober,
    The leaves they were crispèd and sere,
    The leaves they were withering and sere;
It was night in the lonesome October
    Of my most immemorial year;
It was hard by the dim lake of Auber,
    In the misty mid region of Weir,
It was down by the dank tarn of Auber,
    In the ghoul-haunted woodland of Weir.

Here once, through an alley Titanic,
    Of cypress, I roamed with my Soul,
    Of cypress, with Psyche, my Soul.
These were days when my heart was volcanic
    As the scoriac rivers that roll,
    As the lavas that restlessly roll
Their sulphurous currents down Yaanek
    In the ultimate climes of the pole,
That groan as they roll down Mount Yaanek
    In the realms of the boreal pole.

ULALUME

" Here once through an alley Titanic
Of cypress, I roamed with my Soul,
Of cypress, with Psyche, my Soul."

Ulalume

Our talk had been serious and sober,
    But our thoughts they were palsied and sere,
    Our memories were treacherous and sere,
For we knew not the month was October,
    And we marked not the night of the year
    (Ah, night of all nights in the year!);
We noted not the dim lake of Auber
    (Though once we had journeyed down here),
Remembered not the dank tarn of Auber,
    Nor the ghoul-haunted woodland of Weir.

And now, as the night was senescent
    And star-dials pointed to morn,
    As the star-dials hinted of morn,
At the end of our path a liquescent
    And nebulous lustre was born,
Out of which a miraculous crescent
    Arose with a duplicate horn,
Astarte's bediamonded crescent
    Distinct with its duplicate horn.
And I said: " She is warmer than Dian;
    She rolls through an ether of sighs,
    She revels in a region of sighs:

She has seen that the tears are not dry on
    These cheeks, where the worm never dies,
And has come past the stars of the Lion
    To point us the path to the skies,
    To the Lethean peace of the skies;

Ulalume

Come up, in despite of the Lion,
    To shine on us with her bright eyes,
Come up through the lair of the Lion,
    With love in her luminous eyes."

But Psyche, uplifting her finger,
    Said: " Sadly this star I mistrust,
    Her pallor I strangely mistrust;
Oh, hasten! oh, let us not linger!
    Oh, fly! let us fly! for we must."
In terror she spoke, letting sink her
    Wings until they trailed in the dust;
In agony sobbed, letting sink her
    Plumes till they trailed in the dust,
    Till they sorrowfully trailed in the dust.

I replied: " This is nothing but dreaming:
    Let us on by this tremulous light!
    Let us bathe in this crystalline light!
Its sibyllic splendor is beaming
    With hope and in beauty to-night!
    See, it flickers up the sky through the night!
Ah, we safely may trust to its gleaming,
    And be sure it will lead us aright;
We safely may trust to a gleaming
    That cannot but guide us aright,
    Since it flickers up to heaven through the night."

Ulalume

Thus I pacified Psyche and kissed her,
    And tempted her out of her gloom,
    And conquered her scruples and gloom;
And we passed to the end of the vista,
    But were stopped by the door of a tomb,
    By the door of a legended tomb;
And I said: " What is written, sweet sister,
    On the door of this legended tomb ? "
    She replied: " Ulalume! Ulalume!
    'T is the vault of thy lost Ulalume! "

Then my heart it grew ashen and sober
    As the leaves that were crispèd and sere,
    As the leaves that were withering and sere,
And I cried: " It was surely October
    On this very night of last year
    That I journeyed, I journeyed down here,
    That I brought a dread burden down here,
    On this night of all nights in the year,
    Ah, what demon has tempted me here ?
Well I know, now, this dim lake of Auber,
    This misty mid region of Weir,
Well I know, now, this dank tarn of Auber,
    This ghoul-haunted woodland of Weir."

To ___ ___

NOT long ago, the writer of these lines,
    In the mad pride of intellectuality,
    Maintained " the power of words "; denied
   that ever
A thought arose within the human brain
Beyond the utterance of the human tongue:
And now, as if in mockery of that boast,
Two words, two foreign soft disyllables,
Italian tones, made only to be murmured
By angels dreaming in the moonlit " dew
That hangs like chains of pearl on Hermon hill,"
Have stirred from out the abysses of his heart
Unthought-like thoughts that are the souls of thought,
Richer, far wilder, far diviner visions
Than even the seraph harper, Israfel
(Who has " the sweetest voice of all God's creatures "),
Could hope to utter.   And I! my spells are broken.
The pen falls powerless from my shivering hand.
With thy dear name as text, though bidden by thee,
I cannot write; I cannot speak or think;

To ——— ———

Alas! I cannot feel; for 't is not feeling,
This standing motionless upon the golden
Threshold of the wide-open gate of dreams,
Gazing, entranced, adown the gorgeous vista,
And thrilling as I see, upon the right,
Upon the left, and all the way along,
Amid empurpled vapors, far away
To where the prospect terminates—thee only.

An Enigma

"SELDOM we find," says Solomon Don
    Dunce,
    " Half an idea in the profoundest sonnet.
Through all the flimsy things we see at once
    As easily as through a Naples bonnet—
    Trash of all trash! how can a lady don it ?
Yet heavier far than your Petrarchan stuff—
Owl-downy nonsense that the faintest puff
    Twirls into trunk-paper the while you con it."
And, veritably, Sol is right enough.
The general tuckermanities are arrant
Bubbles, ephemeral and so transparent;
    But this is, now—you may depend upon it—
Stable, opaque, immortal—all by dint
Of the dear names that lie concealed within 't.

TO HELEN

"Clad all in white, upon a velvet bank
I saw thee half reclining."

To Helen

I SAW thee once, once only, years ago;
 I must not say how many, but not many.
 It was a July midnight; and from out
A full-orbed moon, that, like thine own soul, soaring,
Sought a precipitate pathway up through heaven,
There fell a silvery-silken veil of light,
With quietude, and sultriness, and slumber,
Upon the upturned faces of a thousand
Roses that grew in an enchanted garden,
Where no wind dared to stir, unless on tiptoe;
Fell on the upturned faces of these roses
That gave out, in return for the love-light,
Their odorous souls in an ecstatic death;
Fell on the upturned faces of these roses
That smiled and died in this parterre, enchanted
By thee, and by the poetry of thy presence.

Clad all in white, upon a violet bank
I saw thee half reclining; while the moon

To Helen

Fell on the upturned faces of the roses,
And on thine own, upturned—alas, in sorrow!

Was it not Fate that, on this July midnight—
Was it not Fate (whose name is also Sorrow),
That bade me pause before that garden-gate,
To breathe the incense of those slumbering roses?
No footstep stirred; the hated world all slept,
Save only thee and me.   (O heaven! O God!
How my heart beats in coupling those two words!)
Save only thee and me.   I paused, I looked,
And in an instant all things disappeared.
(Ah, bear in mind this garden was enchanted!)

The pearly lustre of the moon went out;
The mossy banks and the meandering paths,
The happy flowers and the repining trees,
Were seen no more: the very roses' odors
Died in the arms of the adoring airs.
All, all expired save thee, save less than thou:
Save only the divine light in thine eyes,
Save but the soul in thine uplifted eyes.
I saw but them; they were the world to me.
I saw but them; saw only them for hours;
Saw only them until the moon went down.
What wild heart-histories seemed to lie enwritten
Upon those crystalline, celestial spheres!
How dark a woe! yet how sublime a hope!

To Helen

How silently serene a sea of pride!
How daring an ambition, yet how deep!
How fathomless a capacity for love!

But now, at length, dear Dian sank from sight,
Into a western couch of thunder-cloud;
And thou, a ghost, amid the entombing trees
Didst glide away.   Only thine eyes remained.
They would *not* go; they never yet have gone.
Lighting my lonely pathway home that night,
They have not left me (as my hopes have) since.
They follow me; they lead me through the years.
They are my ministers, yet I their slave.
Their office is to illumine and enkindle;
My duty, to be saved by their bright light,
And purified in their electric fire,
And sanctified in their Elysian fire.
They fill my soul with beauty (which is hope),
And are far up in heaven—the stars I kneel to
In the sad, silent watches of my night;
While even in the meridian glare of day
I see them still, two sweetly scintillant
Venuses, unextinguished by the sun!

150

A Valentine

FOR her this rhyme is penned, whose luminous
		eyes,
	Brightly expressive as the twins of Leda,
Shall find her own sweet name, that, nestling lies
	Upon the page, enwrapped from every reader.
Search narrowly the lines!—they hold a treasure
	Divine, a talisman, an amulet
That must be worn at heart.   Search well the measure,
	The words, the syllables! Do not forget
The trivialest point, or you may lose your labor!
	And yet there is in this no Gordian knot
Which one might not undo without a sabre,
	If one could merely comprehend the plot.
Enwritten upon the leaf where now are peering
	Eyes' scintillating soul, there lie *perdus*
Three eloquent words oft uttered in the hearing
	Of poets, by poets, as the name is a poet's too.
Its letters, although naturally lying
	Like the knight Pinto—Mendez Ferdinando—

A Valentine

Still form a synonym for Truth.   Cease trying!
   You will not read the riddle, though you do the best
      you can do.

[To translate the address, read the first letter of the
first line in connection with the second letter of the
second line, the third letter of the third line, the fourth
of the fourth, and so on to the end.   The name will
thus appear.]

The Bells

I

HEAR the sledges with the bells,
Silver bells!
What a world of merriment their
melody foretells!
How they tinkle, tinkle, tinkle,
In the icy air of night!
While the stars that oversprinkle
All the heavens seem to twinkle
With a crystalline delight;
Keeping time, time, time,
In a sort of Runic rhyme,
To the tintinnabulation that so musically wells
From the bells, bells, bells, bells,
Bells, bells, bells—
From the jingling and the tinkling of the bells.

The Bells

Hear the mellow wedding bells,
Golden bells!
What a world of happiness their harmony foretells!
Through the balmy air of night
How they ring out their delight!
From the molten-golden notes,
And all in tune,
What a liquid ditty floats
To the turtle-dove that listens, while she gloats
On the moon!
Oh, from out the sounding cells
What a gush of euphony voluminously wells!
How it swells!
How it dwells
On the future! how it tells
Of the rapture that impels
To the swinging and the ringing
Of the bells, bells, bells,
Of the bells, bells, bells, bells,
Bells, bells, bells—
To the rhyming and the chiming of the bells!

III

Hear the loud alarum bells—
Brazen bells!
What a tale of terror, now, their turbulency tells!

The Bells

In the startled ear of night
How they scream out their affright!
  Too much horrified to speak,
  They can only shriek, shriek,
    Out of tune,
In a clamorous appealing to the mercy of the fire,
In a mad expostulation with the deaf and frantic fire,
    Leaping higher, higher, higher,
    With a desperate desire
    And a resolute endeavor
    Now, now to sit, or never,
  By the side of the pale-faced moon.
    Oh, the bells, bells, bells!
    What a tale their terror tells
      Of despair!
  How they clang, and clash, and roar!
  What a horror they outpour
On the bosom of the palpitating air!
    Yet the ear it fully knows
      By the twanging
      And the clanging
    How the danger ebbs and flows;
    Yet the ear distinctly tells
      In the jangling
      And the wrangling
    How the danger sinks and swells,
By the sinking or the swelling in the anger of the bells;
    Of the bells—

The Bells

Of the bells, bells, bells bells,
Bells, bells, bells—
In the clamor and the clangor of the bells!

IV

Hear the tolling of the bells,
Iron bells!
What a world of solemn thought their melody compels!
In the silence of the night
How we shiver with affright
At the melancholy menace of their tone!
For every sound that floats
From the rust within their throats
Is a groan.
And the people—ah, the people,
They that dwell up in the steeple
All alone,
And who tolling, tolling, tolling,
In that muffled monotone,
Feel a glory in so rolling
On the human heart a stone—
They are neither man nor woman,
They are neither brute nor human,
They are ghouls;
And their king it is who tolls;
And he rolls, rolls, rolls,
Rolls
A pæan from the bells!

The Bells

And his merry bosom swells
　With the pæan of the bells!
And he dances, and he yells;
Keeping time, time, time,
In a sort of Runic rhyme,
　To the pæan of the bells,
　　Of the bells;
Keeping time, time, time,
In a sort of Runic rhyme,
　To the throbbing of the bells;
Of the bells, bells, bells—
　To the sobbing of the bells;
Keeping time, time, time,
　As he knells, knells, knells,
In a happy Runic rhyme,
　To the rolling of the bells:
Of the bells, bells, bells—
　To the tolling of the bells;
Of the bells, bells, bells, bells,
　Bells, bells, bells—
To the moaning and the groaning of the bells.

Annabel Lee

IT was many and many a year ago,
    In a kingdom by the sea,
    That a maiden there lived whom you may
    know
    By the name of Annabel Lee;
And this maiden she lived with no other thought
    Than to love and be loved by me.

I was a child and she was a child,
    In this kingdom by the sea:
But we loved with a love that was more than love—
    I and my Annabel Lee;
With a love that the winged seraphs of heaven
    Coveted her and me.

And this was the reason that, long ago,
    In this kingdom by the sea,
A wind blew out of a cloud, chilling
    My beautiful Annabel Lee;
So that her high-born kinsman came

Annabel Lee

And bore her away from me,
To shut her up in a sepulchre
   In this kingdom by the sea.

The angels, not half so happy in heaven,
   Went envying her and me;
Yes, that was the reason (as all men know,
   In this kingdom by the sea)
That the wind came out of the cloud by night,
   Chilling and killing my Annabel Lee.

But our love it was stronger by far than the love
   Of those who were older than we,
   Of many far wiser than we;
And neither the angels in heaven above
   Nor the demons down under the sea
Can ever dissever my soul from the soul
   Of the beautiful Annabel Lee;

For the moon never beams without bringing me
   dreams
   Of the beautiful Annabel Lee;
And the stars never rise but I feel the bright eyes
   Of the beautiful Annabel Lee;
And so, all the night-tide, I lie down by the side
Of my darling, my darling, my life and my bride,
   In the sepulchre there by the sea,
   In her tomb by the sounding sea.

ANNABEL LEE

" And so, all the night-tide, I lie down by the side
Of my darling—my darling—my life and my bride,
In her sepulchre there by the sea,
In her tomb by the sounding sea."

To My Mother

BECAUSE I feel that, in the heavens above,
 The angels, whispering to one another,
 Can find, among their burning terms of
 love,
 None so devotional as that of " Mother,"
Therefore by that dear name I long have called you,
 You who are more than mother unto me,
And fill my heart of hearts, where Death installed you,
 In setting my Virginia's spirit free.
My mother—my own mother, who died early,
 Was but the mother of myself; but you
Are mother to the one I loved so dearly,
 And thus are dearer than the mother I knew
By that infinity with which my wife
Was dearer to my soul than its soul-life.

For Annie

THANK Heaven! the crisis—
  The danger is past,
And the lingering illness
  Is over at last,
And the fever called "Living"
  Is conquered at last.

Sadly I know
  I am shorn of my strength,
And no muscle I move
  As I lie at full length;
But no matter! I feel
  I am better at length.

And I rest so composed,
  Now, in my bed,
That any beholder
  Might fancy me dead—
Might start at beholding me,
  Thinking me dead.

For Annie

The moaning and groaning,
　The sighing and sobbing,
Are quieted now,
　With that horrible throbbing
At heart—ah, that horrible,
　Horrible throbbing!
The sickness, the nausea,
　The pitiless pain,
Have ceased, with the fever
　That maddened my brain,
With the fever called " Living "
　That burned in my brain.

And oh! of all tortures
　That torture the worst
Has abated—the terrible
　Torture of thirst
For the naphthaline river
　Of Passion accurst;
I have drunk of a water
　That quenches all thirst:

Of a water that flows,
　With a lullaby sound,
From a spring but a very few
　Feet under ground,
From a cavern not very far
　Down under ground.

VOL. I.—10.

163

For Annie

And ah! let it never
   Be foolishly said
That my room it is gloomy
   And narrow my bed;
For man never slept
   In a different bed—
And, to sleep, you must slumber
   In just such a bed.

My tantalized spirit
   Here blandly reposes,
Forgetting, or never
   Regretting, its roses—
Its old agitations
   Of myrtles and roses;

For now, while so quietly
   Lying, it fancies
A holier odor
   About it, of pansies—
A rosemary odor,
   Commingled with pansies,
With rue and the beautiful
   Puritan pansies.

And so it lies happily,
   Bathing in many
A dream of the truth

For Annie

And the beauty of Annie,
Drowned in a bath
  Of the tresses of Annie.

She tenderly kissed me,
  She fondly caressed,
And then I fell gently
  To sleep on her breast,
Deeply to sleep
  From the heaven of her breast.

When the light was extinguished
  She covered me warm,
And she prayed to the angels
  To keep me from harm,
To the queen of the angels
  To shield me from harm.

And I lie so composedly
  Now in my bed,
(Knowing her love)
  That you fancy me dead;
And I rest so contentedly
  Now in my bed,
(With her love at my breast)
  That you fancy me dead—
That you shudder to look at me,
  Thinking me dead.

For Annie

But my heart is brighter
  Than all of the many
Stars in the sky,
  For it sparkles with Annie—
It glows with the light
  Of the love of my Annie,
With the thought of the light
  Of the eyes of my Annie.

ELDORADO

Eldorado

GAILY bedight,
　A gallant knight,
　　In sunshine and in shadow,
　Had journeyed long,
　Singing a song,
In search of Eldorado.

　But he grew old,
　This knight so bold,
And o'er his heart a shadow
　Fell as he found
　No spot of ground
That looked like Eldorado.

　And, as his strength
　Failed him at length,
He met a pilgrim shadow;
　" Shadow," said he,

Eldorado

" Where can it be,
This land of Eldorado ? "

" Over the mountains
Of the moon,
Down the valley of the shadow,
Ride, boldly ride,"
The shade replied,—
" If you seek for Eldorado ! "

THE POET'S ART

The Purpose of Poetry

LETTER TO B——[1]

T has been said that a good critique on a poem may be written by one who is no poet himself. This, according to your idea and mine of poetry, I feel to be false; the less poetical the critic, the less just the critique, and the converse. On this account, and because there are but few B——'s in the world, I would be as much ashamed of the world's good opinion as proud of your own. Another than yourself might here observe: " Shakespeare is in possession of the world's good opinion, and yet Shakespeare is the greatest of poets. It appears then that

---

[1] Printed, with the following note, in the second volume of the *Southern Literary Messenger:* "These detached passages form part of the preface to a small volume printed some years ago for private circulation. They have vigor and much originality; but of course we shall not be called upon to endorse all the writer's opinions."

The Purpose of Poetry

the world judge correctly: why should you be ashamed
of their favorable judgment? " The difficulty lies in
the interpretation of the word *judgment* or *opinion.*
The opinion is the world's, truly, but it may be
called theirs as a man would call a book his, having
bought it: he did not write the book, but it is his;
they did not originate the opinion, but it is theirs. A
fool, for example, thinks Shakespeare a great poet;
yet the fool has never read Shakespeare. But the
fool's neighbor, who is a step higher on the Andes of
the mind, whose head (that is to say, his more exalted
thought) is too far above the fool to be seen or under-
stood, but whose feet (by which I mean his every-day
actions) are sufficiently near to be discerned, and by
means of which that superiority is ascertained, which
but for them would never have been discovered—this
neighbor asserts that Shakespeare is a great poet; the
fool believes him, and it is henceforth his opinion.
This neighbor's own opinion has, in like manner, been
adopted from one above him, and so, ascendingly, to a
few gifted individuals, who kneel around the summit,
beholding, face to face, the master spirit who stands
upon the pinnacle. . . .

You are aware of the great barrier in the path of an
American writer. He is read, if at all, in preference
to the combined and established wit of the world. I
say " established "; for it is with literature as with law
or empire—an established name is an estate in tenure,

The Purpose of Poetry

or a throne in possession. Besides, one might suppose that books, like their authors, improve by travel, their having crossed the sea is, with us, so great a distinction. Our antiquaries abandon time for distance; our very fops glance from the binding to the bottom of the title-page, where the mystic characters which spell London, Paris, or Genoa are precisely so many letters of recommendation. . . .

I mentioned just now a vulgar error as regards criticism. I think the notion that no poet can form a correct estimate of his own writings is another. I remarked before, that in proportion to the poetical talent, would be the justice of the critique upon poetry. Therefore, a bad poet would, I grant, make a false critique, and his self-love would infallibly bias his little judgment in his favor; but a poet, who is indeed a poet, could not, I think, fail of making a just critique. Whatever should be deducted on the score of self-love might be replaced on account of his intimate acquaintance with the subject; in short, we have more instances of false criticism than of just, where one's own writings are the test, simply because we have more bad poets than good. There are, of course, many objections to what I say: Milton is a great example of the contrary; but his opinion with respect to the *Paradise Regained,* is by no means fairly ascertained. By what trivial circumstances men are often led to assert what they do not really believe! Perhaps an inadvertent word has descended to posterity. But, in fact, the *Paradise Regained* is little, if at all, inferior to the *Paradise Lost,* and is only supposed so to be because men do not like epics, whatever they may say to the contrary, and, reading those of Milton in their natural order, are too much wearied with the first to derive any pleasure from the second.

I dare say Milton preferred *Comus* to either; if so, justly. . . .

As I am speaking of poetry, it will not be amiss to touch slightly upon the most singular heresy in its modern history—the heresy of what is called, very foolishly, the Lake School. Some years ago I might have been induced, by an occasion like the present, to attempt a formal refutation of their doctrine; at present it would be a work of supererogation. The wise must bow to the wisdom of such men as Coleridge and Southey, but, being wise, have laughed at poetical theories so prosaically exemplified.

Aristotle, with singular assurance, has declared poetry the most philosophical of all writings,[1] but it required a Wordsworth to pronounce it the most metaphysical. He seems to think that the end of poetry is, or should be, instruction; yet it is a truism that the end of our existence is happiness: if so, the end of every separate part of our existence, everything connected with our existence, should be still, happi-

---

[1] *Spoudiotaton kai philosophikotaton genos.*

The Purpose of Poetry

ness. Therefore the end of instruction should be happiness; and happiness is another name for pleasure; therefore the end of instruction should be pleasure, yet we see the above-mentioned opinion implies precisely the reverse.

To proceed: *ceteris paribus,* he who pleases is of more importance to his fellow-men than he who instructs, since utility is happiness, and pleasure is the end already obtained, which instruction is merely the means of obtaining.

I see no reason, then, why our metaphysical poets should plume themselves so much on the utility of their works, unless, indeed, they refer to instruction with eternity in view; in which case, sincere respect for their piety would not allow me to express my contempt for their judgment, contempt which it would be difficult to conceal, since their writings are professedly to be understood by the few, and it is the many who stand in need of salvation. In such case I should no doubt be tempted to think of the Devil in *Melmoth,* who labors indefatigably through three octavo volumes to accomplish the destruction of one or two souls, while any common devil would have demolished one or two thousand. . . .

Against the subtleties which would make poetry a study, not a passion, it becomes the metaphysician to reason, but the poet to protest. Yet Wordsworth and Coleridge are men in years: the one imbued in contemplation from his childhood; the other, a giant in intellect and learning. The diffidence, then, with which I venture to dispute their authority would be overwhelming, did I not feel, from the bottom of my heart, that learning has little to do with the imagination, intellect with the passions, or age with poetry. . . .

> Trifles, like straws, upon the surface flow,
> He who would search for pearls must dive below,

are lines which have done much mischief. As regards the greater truths, men oftener err by seeking them at the bottom than at the top; the depth lies in the huge abysses where wisdom is sought, not in the palpable palaces where she is found. The ancients were not always right in hiding the goddess in a well: witness the light which Bacon has thrown upon philosophy; witness the principles of our divine faith, that moral mechanism by which the simplicity of a child may overbalance the wisdom of a man.

We see an instance of Coleridge's liability to err, in his *Biographia Literaria,* professedly his literary life and opinions, but, in fact, a treatise *de omni scibili et quibusdam aliis.* He goes wrong by reason of his very profundity, and of his error we have a natural type in the contemplation of a star. He who regards it directly and intensely sees, it is true, the star, but it is the star without a ray; while he who surveys it less inquisitively is conscious of all for which the star is useful to us below, its brilliancy and its beauty. . . .

As to Wordsworth, I have no faith in him. That he had, in youth, the feelings of a poet, I believe, for there are glimpses of extreme delicacy in his writings (and delicacy is the poet's own kingdom, his *El Dorado*), but they have the appearance of a better day recollected; and glimpses, at best, are little evidence of present poetic fire—we know that a few straggling flowers spring up daily in the crevices of the glacier.

He was to blame in wearing away his youth in contemplation with the end of poetizing in his manhood. With the increase of his judgment the light which should make it apparent has faded away. His judgment, consequently, is too correct. This may not be understood; but the old Goths of Germany would have understood it, who used to debate matters of importance to their State twice, once when drunk, and once when sober: sober, that they might not be deficient in formality; drunk, lest they should be destitute of vigor.

The long wordy discussions by which he tries to reason us into admiration of his poetry speak very little in his favor; they are full of such assertions as this (I have opened one of his volumes at random): " Of genius the only proof is the act of doing well what is worthy to be done, and what was never done before." Indeed! then it follows that in doing what is unworthy to be done, or what has been done before, no genius can be evinced; yet the picking of pockets is an unworthy act; pockets have been picked time immemorial, and Barrington, the pickpocket, in point of genius, would have thought hard of a comparison with William Wordsworth, the poet.

Again, in estimating the merit of certain poems, whether they be Ossian's or McPherson's can surely be of little consequence, yet, in order to prove their worthlessness, Mr. W. has expended many pages in the controversy. *Tantaene animis?* Can great minds descend to such absurdity? But worse still: that he may bear down every argument in favor of these poems, he triumphantly drags forward a passage, in his abomination of which he expects the reader to sympathize. It is the beginning of the epic poem, *Temora.* " The blue waves of Ullin roll in light; the green hills are covered with day; trees shake their dusky heads in the breeze." And this—this gorgeous, yet simple imagery, where all is alive and panting with immortality—this, William Wordsworth, the author of *Peter Bell,* has selected for his contempt. We shall see what better he, in his own person, has to offer. Imprimis:

> And now she 's at the pony's head,
> And now she 's at the pony's tail,
> On that side now, and now on this,

The Purpose of Poetry

And almost stifled her with bliss—
A few sad tears does Betty shed,
She pats the pony where or when
She knows not: happy Betty Foy!
Oh, Johnny! never mind the Doctor!

Secondly:—

The dew was falling fast, the—stars began to blink,
I heard a voice; it said: "Drink, pretty creature, drink!"
And, looking o'er the hedge, be—fore me I espied
A snow-white mountain lamb, with a—maiden at its side.
No other sheep were near, the lamb was all alone,
And by a slender cord was—tether'd to a stone.

Now, we have no doubt this is all true; we will believe it; indeed, we will, Mr. W. Is it sympathy for the sheep you wish to excite? I love a sheep from the bottom of my heart. . . .

But there are occasions, dear B——, there are occasions when even Wordsworth is reasonable. Even Stamboul, it is said, shall have an end, and the most unlucky blunders must come to a conclusion. Here is an extract from his preface:

" Those who have been accustomed to the phraseology of modern writers, if they persist in reading this book to a conclusion [impossible!], will, no doubt, have to struggle with feelings of awkwardness [ha! ha! ha!]; they will look round for poetry [ha! ha! ha! ha!], and will be induced to inquire by what species of courtesy these attempts have been permitted to assume that title." [Ha! ha! ha! ha! ha!]

Yet let not Mr. W. despair; he has given immortality to a wagon and the bee; Sophocles has transmitted to eternity a sore toe, and dignified a tragedy with a chorus of turkeys. . . .

Of Coleridge I cannot speak but with reverence. His towering intellect! his gigantic power! He is one more evidence of the fact "que la plupart des sectes ont raison dans une bonne partie de ce qu'elles avancent, mais non pas en ce qu'elles nient." He has imprisoned his own conceptions by the barrier he has erected against those of others. It is lamentable to think that such a mind should be buried in metaphysics, and, like the *Nyctanthes,* waste its perfume upon the night alone. In reading his poetry, I tremble, like one who stands upon a volcano, conscious, from the very darkness bursting from the crater, of the fire and the light that are weltering below.

What is Poetry? Poetry! that Proteus-like idea, with as many appellations as the nine-titled Corcyra! "Give me," I demanded of a scholar some time ago, "give me a definition of poetry." "*Très volontiers*"; and he proceeded to his library, brought me a Dr. Johnson, and overwhelmed me with a definition. Shade of the immortal Shakespeare! I imagine to myself the scowl of your spiritual eye upon the pro-

The Purpose of Poetry

fanity of that scurrilous Ursa Major. Think of poetry, dear B——; think of poetry, and then think of Dr. Samuel Johnson! Think of all that is airy and fairylike, and then of all that is hideous and unwieldy; think of his huge bulk, the elephant! and then—and then think of the *Tempest,* the *Midsummer Night's Dream,*—Prospero, Oberon, and Titania! . . .

A poem, in my opinion, is opposed to a work of science by having, for its immediate object, pleasure, not truth; to romance, by having, for its object, an indefinite instead of a definite pleasure, being a poem only so far as this object is attained; romance presenting perceptible images with definite, poetry with indefinite, sensations, to which end music is an essential, since the comprehension of sweet sound is our most indefinite, conception. Music, when combined with a pleasurable idea, is poetry; music, without the idea, is simply music; the idea, without the music, is prose, from its very definitiveness.

What was meant by the invective against him who had no music in his soul? . . .

To sum up this long rigmarole, I have, dear B——, what you no doubt perceive, for the metaphysical poets, as poets, the most sovereign contempt. That they have followers proves nothing—

> No Indian prince has to his palace
> More followers than a thief to the gallows.

The Poetic Principle

IN speaking of the poetic principle, I have no design to be either thorough or profound. While discussing very much at random the essentiality of what we call poetry, my principal purpose will be to cite for consideration some few of those minor English or American poems which best suit my own taste, or which upon my own fancy have left the most definite impression. By " minor poems " I mean, of course, poems of little length. And here, in the beginning, permit me to say a few words in regard to a somewhat peculiar principle which, whether rightfully or wrongfully, has always had its influence in my own critical estimate of the poem. I hold that a long poem does not exist. I maintain that the phrase, " a long poem," is simply a flat contradiction in terms.

I need scarcely observe that a poem deserves its title only inasmuch as it excites, by elevating the soul.

The Poetic Principle

The value of the poem is in the ratio of this elevating excitement. But all excitements are, through a psychal necessity, transient. That degree of excitement which would entitle a poem to be so called at all, cannot be sustained throughout a composition of any great length. After the lapse of half an hour, at the very utmost, it flags, fails, a revulsion ensues, and then the poem is, in effect and in fact, no longer such.

There are, no doubt, many who have found difficulty in reconciling the critical dictum that the *Paradise Lost* is to be devoutly admired throughout, with the absolute impossibility of maintaining for it, during perusal, the amount of enthusiasm which that critical dictum would demand. This great work, in fact, is to be regarded as poetical, only when, losing sight of that vital requisite in all works of art, unity, we view it merely as a series of minor poems. If, to preserve its unity, its totality of effect or impression, we read it (as would be necessary) at a single sitting, the result is but a constant alternation of excitement and depression. After a passage of what we feel to be true poetry, there follows inevitably a passage of platitude which no critical prejudgment can force us to admire; but if upon completing the work, we read it again, omitting the first book (that is to say, commencing with the second) we shall be surprised at now finding that admirable which we before

The Poetic Principle

condemned, that damnable which we had previously so much admired. It follows from all this that the ultimate, aggregate, or absolute effect of even the best epic under the sun is a nullity:—and this is precisely the fact.

In regard to the *Iliad,* we have, if not positive proof, at least very good reason for believing it intended as a series of lyrics; but, granting the epic intention, I can say only that the work is based on an imperfect sense of art. The modern epic is, of the supposititious ancient model, but an inconsiderate and blindfold imitation. But the day of these artistic anomalies is over. If, at any time, any very long poem were popular in reality, which I doubt, it is at least clear that no very long poem will ever be popular again.

That the extent of a poetical work is, *ceteris paribus,* the measure of its merit, seems undoubtedly, when we thus state it, a proposition sufficiently absurd; yet we are indebted for it to the quarterly reviews. Surely there can be nothing in mere size, abstractly considered there can be nothing in mere bulk, so far as a volume is concerned, which has so continuously elicited admiration from these saturnine pamphlets! A mountain, to be sure, by the mere sentiment of physical magnitude which it conveys, does impress us with a sense of the sublime; but no man is impressed after this fashion by the

The Poetic Principle

material grandeur of even *The Columbiad.* Even the quarterlies have not instructed us to be so impressed by it. As yet, they have not insisted on our estimating Lamartine by the cubic foot, or Pollok by the pound; but what else are we to infer from their continual prating about " sustained effort " ? If by " sustained effort " any little gentleman has accomplished an epic, let us frankly commend him for the effort, if this indeed be a thing commendable; but let us forbear praising the epic on the effort's account. It is to be hoped that common sense, in the time to come, will prefer deciding upon a work of art rather by the impression it makes, by the effect it produces, than by the time it took to impress the effect, or by the amount of " sustained effort " which had been found necessary in effecting the impression. The fact is, that perseverance is one thing and genius quite another, nor can all the quarterlies in Christendom confound them. By and by, this proposition, with many which I have been just urging, will be received as self-evident. In the meantime, by being generally condemned as falsities, they will not be essentially damaged as truths.

On the other hand, it is clear that a poem may be improperly brief. Undue brevity degenerates into mere epigrammatism. A very short poem, while now and then producing a brilliant or vivid, never produces a profound or enduring, effect. There must be the steady pressing down of the stamp upon the wax. De Béranger has wrought innumerable things, pungent and spirit-stirring; but, in general, they have been too imponderous to stamp themselves deeply into the public opinion; and thus, as so many feathers of fancy, have been blown aloft only to be whistled down the wind.

A remarkable instance of the effect of undue brevity in depressing a poem, in keeping it out of the popular view, is afforded by the following exquisite little serenade:

> I arise from dreams of thee
> In the first sweet sleep of night,
> When the winds are breathing low,
> And the stars are shining bright.
> I arise from dreams of thee,
> And a spirit in my feet
> Has led me—who knows how?—
> To thy chamber-window, sweet!
>
> The wandering airs they faint
> On the dark, the silent stream—
> The champak odors fail
> Like sweet thoughts in a dream;
> The nightingale's complaint,
> It dies upon her heart,
> As I must die on thine,
> Oh, beloved as thou art!
>
> Oh, lift me from the grass!
> I die, I faint, I fail!

The Poetic Principle

> Let thy love in kisses rain
>   On my lips and eyelids pale.
> My cheek is cold and white, alas!
>   My heart beats loud and fast,
> Oh, press it close to thine again,
>   Where it will break at last!

Very few, perhaps, are familiar with these lines, yet no less a poet than Shelley is their author. Their warm, yet delicate and ethereal imagination will be appreciated by all, but by none so thoroughly as by him who has himself arisen from sweet dreams of one beloved, to bathe in the aromatic air of a Southern midsummer night.

One of the finest poems by Willis—the very best, in my opinion, which he has ever written—has, no doubt, through this same defect of undue brevity, been kept back from its proper position, not less in the critical than in the popular view.

> The shadows lay along Broadway,
>   'T was near the twilight-tide,
> And slowly there a lady fair
>   Was walking in her pride.
> Alone walked she; but, viewlessly,
>   Walked spirits at her side.
>
> Peace charmed the street beneath her feet,
>   And honor charmed the air;
> And all astir looked kind on her,
>   And call'd her good as fair,

The Poetic Principle

For all God ever gave to her,
　She kept with chary care.

She kept with care her beauties rare
　From lovers warm and true,
For her heart was cold to all but gold,
　And the rich came not to woo;
But honored well are charms to sell
　If priests the selling do.

Now walking there was one more fair,
　A slight girl, lily-pale;
And she had unseen company
　To make the spirit quail:
'Twixt Want and Scorn she walk'd forlorn,
　And nothing could avail.

No mercy now can clear her brow
　For this world's peace to pray;
For, as love's wild prayer dissolved in air,
　Her woman's heart gave way!
But the sin forgiven by Christ in heaven
　By man is cursed alway!

In this composition we find it difficult to recognize the Willis who has written so many mere " verses of society." The lines are not only richly ideal, but full of energy; while they breathe an earnestness, an evident sincerity of sentiment, for which we look in vain throughout all the other works of this author.

While the epic mania, while the idea that, to merit in poetry, prolixity is indispensable, has, for some years past, been gradually dying out of the public

The Poetic Principle

mind, by mere dint of its own absurdity, we find it succeeded by a heresy too palpably false to be long tolerated, but one which, in the brief period it has already endured, may be said to have accomplished more in the corruption of our poetical literature than all its other enemies combined. I allude to the heresy of " The Didactic." It has been assumed, tacitly and avowedly, directly and indirectly, that the ultimate object of all poetry is truth. Every poem, it is said, should inculcate a moral; and by this moral is the poetical merit of the work to be adjudged. We Americans especially have patronized this happy idea; and we Bostonians, very especially, have developed it in full. We have taken it into our heads that to write a poem simply for the poem's sake, and to acknowledge such to have been our design, would be to confess ourselves radically wanting in the true poetic dignity and force: but the simple fact is, that, would we but permit ourselves to look into our own souls, we should immediately there discover that under the sun there neither exists nor can exist any work more thoroughly dignified, more supremely noble than this very poem, this poem *per se,* this poem which is a poem and nothing more, this poem written solely for the poem's sake.

With as deep a reverence for the true as ever inspired the bosom of man, I would, nevertheless limit, in some measure, its modes of inculcation. I would

The Poetic Principle

limit to enforce them. I would not enfeeble them by
dissipation. The demands of Truth are severe; she
has no sympathy with the myrtles. All that which is
so indispensable in song is precisely all that with
which she has nothing whatever to do. It is but mak-
ing her a flaunting paradox, to wreathe her in gems and
flowers. In enforcing a truth, we need severity rather
than efflorescence of language. We must be simple,
precise, terse. We must be cool, calm, unimpas-
sioned. In a word, we must be in that mood which,
as nearly as possible, is the exact converse of the poet-
ical. He must be blind indeed who does not perceive
the radical and chasmal differences between the truth-
ful and the poetical modes of inculcation. He must
be theory-mad beyond redemption who, in spite of
these differences, shall still persist in attempting to
reconcile the obstinate oils and waters of poetry and
truth.

Dividing the world of mind into its three most im-
mediately obvious distinctions, we have the pure intel-
lect, taste, and the moral sense. I place taste in the
middle, because it is just this position which, in the
mind, it occupies. It holds intimate relations with
either extreme, but from the moral sense is separated
by so faint a difference that Aristotle has not hesitated
to place some of its operations among the virtues
themselves. Nevertheless, we find the offices of the
trio marked with a sufficient distinction. Just as the

The Poetic Principle

intellect concerns itself with truth, so taste informs us of the beautiful, while the moral sense is regardful of duty. Of this latter, while conscience teaches the obligation, and reason the expediency, taste contents herself with displaying the charms, waging war upon vice solely on the ground of her deformity, her disproportion, her animosity to the fitting, to the appropriate, to the harmonious—in a word, to beauty.

An immortal instinct, deep within the spirit of man, is thus, plainly, a sense of the beautiful. This it is which administers to his delight in the manifold forms, and sounds, and odors, and sentiments amid which he exists. And just as the lily is repeated in the lake, or the eyes of Amaryllis in the mirror, so is the mere oral or written repetition of these forms, and sounds, and colors, and odors, and sentiments a duplicate source of delight. But this mere repetition is not poetry. He who shall simply sing, with however glowing enthusiasm, or with however vivid a truth of description, of the sights, and sounds, and odors, and colors, and sentiments which greet him in common with all mankind—he, I say, has yet failed to prove his divine title. There is still a something in the distance which he has been unable to attain. We have still a thirst unquenchable, to allay which he has not shown us the crystal springs. This thirst belongs to the immortality of man. It is at once a consequence and an indication of his perennial existence. It is the

The Poetic Principle

desire of the moth for the star. It is no mere appreciation of the beauty before us, but a wild effort to reach the beauty above. Inspired by an ecstatic prescience of the glories beyond the grave, we struggle, by multiform combinations among the things and thoughts of time, to attain a portion of that loveliness whose very elements, perhaps, appertain to eternity alone. And thus when by poetry, or when by music, the most entrancing of the poetic moods, we find ourselves melted into tears, not as the Abbaté Gravia supposes, through excess of pleasure, but through a certain petulant, impatient sorrow at our inability to grasp now wholly, here on earth, at once and forever, those divine and rapturous joys, of which through the poem, or through the music, we attain to but brief and indeterminate glimpses.

The struggle to apprehend the supernal loveliness, this struggle on the part of souls fittingly constituted, has given to the world all that which it (the world) has ever been enabled at once to understand and to feel as poetic.

The poetic sentiment, of course, may develop itself in various modes: in painting, in sculpture, in architecture, in the dance, very especially in music, and very peculiarly and with a wide field, in the composition of the landscape garden. Our present theme, however, has regard only to its manifestation in words. And here let me speak briefly on the topic of

The Poetic Principle

rhythm. Contenting myself with the certainty that music in its various modes of metre, rhythm, and rhyme, is of so vast a moment in poetry as never to be wisely rejected; is so vitally important an adjunct that he is simply silly who declines its assistance, I will not now pause to maintain its absolute essentiality. It is in music, perhaps, that the soul most nearly attains the great end for which, when inspired by the poetic sentiment, it struggles—the creation of supernal beauty. It may be, indeed, that here this sublime end is, now and then, attained in fact. We are often made to feel, with a shivering delight, that from an earthly harp are stricken notes which cannot have been unfamiliar to the angels. And thus there can be little doubt that in the union of poetry with music in its popular sense we shall find the widest field for the poetic development. The old Bards and Minnesingers had advantages which we do not possess, and Thomas Moore, singing his own songs, was, in the most legitimate manner, perfecting them as poems.

To recapitulate, then: I would define, in brief, the poetry of words as "the rhythmical creation of beauty." Its sole arbiter is taste. With the intellect or with the conscience it has only collateral relations. Unless incidentally, it has no concern whatever either with duty or with truth.

A few words, however, in explanation. That pleasure which is at once the most pure, the most elevating,

The Poetic Principle

and the most intense, is derived, I maintain, from the contemplation of the beautiful. In the contemplation of beauty we alone find it possible to attain that pleasurable elevation, or excitement, of the soul, which we recognize as the poetic sentiment, and which is so easily distinguished from truth, which is the satisfaction of the reason, or from passion, which is the excitement of the heart. I make beauty, there-fore,—using the word as inclusive of the sublime,—I make beauty the province of the poem, simply be-cause it is an obvious rule of art that effects should be made to spring as directly as possible from their causes, no one as yet having been weak enough to deny that the peculiar elevation in question is at least most readily attainable in the poem. It by no means follows, however, that the incitements of pas-sion, or the precepts of duty, or even the lessons of truth, may not be introduced into a poem, and with advantage; for they may subserve, incidentally, in various ways, the general purposes of the work; but the true artist will always contrive to tone them down in proper subjection to that beauty which is the atmos-phere and the real essence of the poem.

I cannot better introduce the few poems which I shall present for your consideration than by the cita-tion of the proem to Mr. Longfellow's *Waif:*

> The day is done, and the darkness
> Falls from the wings of night,

The Poetic Principle

As a feather is wafted downward
  From an eagle in his flight.

I see the lights of the village
  Gleam through the rain and the mist,
And a feeling of sadness comes o'er me,
  That my soul cannot resist;

A feeling of sadness and longing,
  That is not akin to pain,
And resembles sorrow only
  As the mist resembles the rain.

Come, read to me some poem,
  Some simple and heartfelt lay,
That shall soothe this restless feeling
  And banish the thoughts of day.

Not from the grand old masters,
  Not from the bards sublime,
Whose distant footsteps echo
  Through the corridors of time.

For, like strains of martial music,
  Their mighty thoughts suggest
Life's endless toil and endeavor;
  And to-night I long for rest.

Read from some humbler poet,
  Whose songs gushed from his heart,
As showers from the clouds of summer,
  Or tears from the eyelids start;

Who through long days of labor,
  And nights devoid of ease,
Still heard in his soul the music
  Of wonderful melodies.

The Poetic Principle

Such songs have power to quiet
  The restless pulse of care,
And come like the benediction
  That follows after prayer.

Then read from the treasured volume
  The poem of thy choice,
And lend to the rhyme of the poet
  The beauty of thy voice.

And the night shall be filled with music,
  And the cares that infest the day,
Shall fold their tents, like the Arabs,
  And as silently steal away.

With no great range of imagination, these lines have been justly admired for their delicacy of expression. Some of the images are very effective. Nothing can be better than

   . . . the bards sublime,
Whose distant footsteps echo
  Through the corridors of time.

The idea of the last quatrain is also very effective. The poem, on the whole, however, is chiefly to be admired for the graceful *insouciance* of its metre, so well in accordance with the character of the sentiments, and especially for the ease of the general manner. This " ease," or naturalness, in a literary style, it has long been the fashion to regard as ease in appearance alone, as a point of really difficult attainment.

The Poetic Principle

But not so; a natural manner is difficult only to him who should never meddle with it—to the unnatural. It is but the result of writing with the understanding, or with the instinct, that the tone in composition should always be that which the mass of mankind would adopt, and must perpetually vary, of course, with the occasion. The author who, after the fashion of the *North American Review,* should be, upon all occasions, merely " quiet," must necessarily, upon many occasions, be simply silly or stupid, and has no more right to be considered " easy " or " natural " than a cockney exquisite, or than the Sleeping Beauty in the wax-works.

Among the minor poems of Bryant, none has so much impressed me as the one which he entitles *June.* I quote only a portion of it:

> There, through the long, long summer hours,
>   The golden light should lie,
> And thick, young herbs and groups of flowers
>   Stand in their beauty by.
> The oriole should build and tell
> His love-tale, close beside my cell;
>   The idle butterfly
> Should rest him there, and there be heard
> The housewife-bee and humming-bird.
>
> And what if cheerful shouts, at noon,
>   Come, from the village sent,
> Or songs of maids, beneath the moon,
>   With fairy laughter blent ?

The Poetic Principle

And what if, in the evening light,
Betrothèd lovers walk in sight
    Of my low monument ?
I would the lovely scene around
Might know no sadder sight nor sound.

I know, I know I should not see
    The season's glorious show,
Nor would its brightness shine for me,
    Nor its wild music flow;
But if, around my place of sleep,
The friends I love should come to weep,
    They might not haste to go.
Soft airs, and song, and light, and bloom
Should keep them, lingering by my tomb.

These to their soften'd hearts should bear
    The thought of what has been,
And speak of one who cannot share
    The gladness of the scene;
Whose part in all the pomp that fills
The circuit of the summer hills,
    Is—that his grave is green;
And deeply would their hearts rejoice
To hear again his living voice.

The rhythmical flow here is even voluptuous, nothing could be more melodious. The poem has always affected me in a remarkable manner. The intense melancholy which seems to well up, perforce, to the surface of all the poet's cheerful sayings about his grave, we find thrilling us to the soul, while there is

The Poetic Principle

the truest poetic elevation in the thrill. The impression left is one of a pleasurable sadness. And if, in the remaining compositions which I shall introduce to you, there be more or less of a similar tone always apparent, let me remind you that (how or why we know not) this certain taint of sadness is inseparably connected with all the higher manifestations of true beauty. It is, nevertheless,

> A feeling of sadness and longing,
>   That is not akin to pain,
> And resembles sorrow only
>   As the mist resembles the rain.

The taint of which I speak is clearly perceptible even in a poem so full of brilliancy and spirit as the *Health* of Edward C. Pinkney:

> I fill this cup to one made up
>   Of loveliness alone,
> A woman, of her gentle sex
>   The seeming paragon;
> To whom the better elements
>   And kindly stars have given
> A form so fair, that, like the air,
>   'T is less of earth than heaven.
>
> Her every tone is music's own,
>   Like those of morning birds,
> And something more than melody
>   Dwells ever in her words:

The Poetic Principle

The coinage of her heart are they,
   And from her lips each flows
As one may see the burden'd bee
   Forth issue from the rose.

Affections are as thoughts to her,
   The measures of her hours;
Her feelings have the fragrancy,
   The freshness of young flowers;
And lovely passions, changing oft,
   So fill her, she appears
The image of themselves by turns,—
   The idol of past years!

Of her bright face one glance will trace
   A picture on the brain,
And of her voice in echoing hearts
   A sound must long remain;
But memory, such as mine of her,
   So very much endears,
When death is nigh my latest sigh
   Will not be life's, but hers.

I fill'd this cup to one made up
   Of loveliness alone,
A woman, of her gentle sex
   The seeming paragon—
Her health! and would on earth there stood
   Some more of such a frame,
That life might be all poetry,
   And weariness a name.

It was the misfortune of Mr. Pinkney to have been
born too far south. Had he been a New Englander, it

The Poetic Principle

is probable that he would have been ranked as the first of American lyrists by that magnanimous cabal which has so long controlled the destinies of American Letters in conducting the thing called the *North American Review.* The poem just cited is especially beautiful; but the poetic elevation which it induces we must refer chiefly to our sympathy in the poet's enthusiasm. We pardon his hyperboles for the evident earnestness with which they are uttered.

It is by no means my design, however, to expatiate upon the merits of what I should read you. These will necessarily speak for themselves. Boccalini, in his *Advertisements from Parnassus,* tells us that Zoilus once presented Apollo a very caustic criticism upon a very admirable book, whereupon the god asked him for the beauties of the work. He replied that he only busied himself about the errors. On hearing this, Apollo, handing him a sack of unwinnowed wheat, bade him pick out all the chaff for his reward.

Now, this fable answers very well as a hit at the critics, but I am by no means sure that the god was in the right. I am by no means certain that the true limits of the critical duty are not grossly misunderstood. Excellence, in a poem especially, may be considered in the light of an axiom, which need only be properly put to become self-evident. It is not excellence if it requires to be demonstrated as such; and thus, to point out too particularly the merits of

The Poetic Principle

a work of art is to admit that they are not merits altogether.

Among the *Melodies* of Thomas Moore is one whose distinguished character as a poem proper seems to have been singularly left out of view. I allude to his lines beginning, " Come, rest in this bosom." The intense energy of their expression is not surpassed by anything in Byron. There are two of the lines in which a sentiment is conveyed that embodies the all-in-all of the divine passion of love—a sentiment which, perhaps, has found its echo in more, and in more passionate, human hearts than any other single sentiment ever embodied in words:

Come, rest in this bosom, my own stricken deer,
Though the herd have fled from thee, thy home is still here;
Here still is the smile that no cloud can o'ercast,
And a heart and a hand all thy own to the last.

Oh! what was love made for, if 't is not the same
Through joy and through torment, through glory and shame?
I know not, I ask not, if guilt 's in that heart,
I but know that I love thee, whatever thou art.

Thou hast call'd me thy Angel in moments of bliss.
And thy Angel I 'll be, 'mid the horrors of this,
Through the furnace, unshrinking, thy steps to pursue,
And shield thee, and save thee,—or perish there too!

It has been the fashion, of late days, to deny Moore imagination while granting him fancy—a distinction

The Poetic Principle

originating with Coleridge, than whom no man more fully comprehended the great powers of Moore. The fact is, that the fancy of this poet so far predominates over all his other faculties and over the fancy of all other men, as to have induced, very naturally, the idea that he is fanciful only. But never was there a greater mistake. Never was a grosser wrong done the fame of a true poet. In the compass of the English language I can call to mind no poem more profoundly, more weirdly imaginative, in the best sense, than the lines commencing, " I would I were by that dim lake," which are the composition of Thomas Moore. I regret that I am unable to remember them.

One of the noblest, and, speaking of fancy, one of the most singularly fanciful, of modern poets was Thomas Hood. His *Fair Ines* had always for me an inexpressible charm:

> Oh! saw ye not fair Ines ?
>   She 's gone into the West,
> To dazzle when the sun is down,
>   And rob the world of rest:
> She took our daylight with her,
>   The smiles that we love best,
> With morning blushes on her cheek,
>   And pearls upon her breast.
>
> Oh! turn again, fair Ines,
>   Before the fall of night,

The Poetic Principle

For fear the moon should shine alone,
   And stars unrivall'd bright;
And blessèd will the lover be
   That walks beneath their light,
And breathes the love against thy cheek
   I dare not even write!

Would I had been, fair Ines,
   That gallant cavalier,
Who rode so gayly by thy side,
   And whispered thee so near!
Were there no bonny dames at home,
   Or no true lovers here,
That he should cross the seas to win
   The dearest of the dear?

I saw thee, lovely Ines,
   Descend along the shore,
With bands of noble gentlemen,
   And banners waved before;
And gentle youth and maidens gay,
   And snowy plumes they wore;
It would have been a beauteous dream,
   —If it had been no more!

Alas, alas, fair Ines!
   She went away with song,
With Music waiting on her steps,
   And shoutings of the throng;
But some were sad and felt no mirth,
   But only Music's wrong,
In sounds that sang Farewell, Farewell,
   To her you 've loved so long.

The Poetic Principle

Farewell, farewell, fair Ines,
   That vessel never bore
So fair a lady on its deck,
   Nor danced so light before.
Alas for pleasure on the sea,
   And sorrow on the shore!
The smile that blessed one lover's heart
   Has broken many more.

The *Haunted House,* by the same author, is one of the truest poems ever written, one of the truest, one of the most unexceptionable, one of the most thoroughly artistic, both in its theme and in its execution. It is, moreover, powerfully ideal—imaginative. I regret that its length renders it unsuitable for the purposes of this lecture. In place of it permit me to offer the universally appreciated *Bridge of Sighs:*

One more unfortunate,
Weary of breath,
Rashly importunate,
Gone to her death!

Take her up tenderly,
Lift her with care;
Fashion'd so slenderly,
Young, and so fair!

Look at her garments
Clinging like cerements;
Whilst the wave constantly
Drips from her clothing;

The Poetic Principle

Take her up instantly,
Loving, not loathing.

Touch her not scornfully;
Think of her mournfully,
Gently and humanly;
Not of the stains of her,
All that remains of her
Now, is pure womanly.

Make no deep scrutiny
Into her mutiny
Rash and undutiful:
Past all dishonor,
Death has left on her
Only the beautiful.

Still, for all slips of hers,
One of Eve's family—
Wipe those poor lips of hers
Oozing so clammily;

Loop up her tresses
Escaped from the comb,
Her fair auburn tresses;
Whilst wonderment guesses
Where was her home?

Who was her father?
Who was her mother?
Had she a sister?
Had she a brother?
Or was there a dearer one
Still, and a nearer one
Yet, than all other?

The Poetic Principle

Alas! for the rarity
Of Christian charity
Under the sun!
Oh, it was pitiful!
Near a whole city full,
Home she had none.

Sisterly, brotherly,
Fatherly, motherly
Feelings had changed:
Love, by harsh evidence
Thrown from its eminence;
Even God's providence
Seeming estranged.

Where the lamps quiver
So far in the river,
With many a light
From window and casement,
From garret to basement,
She stood, with amazement,
Houseless by night.

The bleak wind of March
Made her tremble and shiver;
But not the dark arch,
Or the black flowing river:
Mad from life's history,
Glad to death's mystery,
Swift to be hurl'd—
Anywhere, anywhere
Out of the world!

The Poetic Principle

In she plunged boldly,
No matter how coldly
The rough river ran,—
Over the brink of it,
Picture it--think of it,
Dissolute man!
Lave in it, drink of it,
Then, if you can!

Take her up tenderly,
Lift her with care;
Fashion'd so slenderly,
Young, and so fair!

Ere her limbs frigidly
Stiffen too rigidly,
Decently, kindly,
Smooth, and compose them;
And her eyes, close them,
Staring so blindly!

Dreadfully staring
Through muddy impurity,
As when with the daring
Last look of despairing
Fixed on futurity.

Perishing gloomily,
Spurred by contumely,
Cold inhumanity,
Burning insanity,
Into her rest.
Cross her hands humbly,

The Poetic Principle

As if praying dumbly,
Over her breast!

Owning her weakness,
Her evil behavior,
And leaving, with meekness,
Her sins to her Saviour!

The vigor of this poem is no less remarkable than its pathos. The versification, although carrying the fanciful to the very verge of the fantastic, is nevertheless admirably adapted to the wild insanity which is the thesis of the poem.

Among the minor poems of Lord Byron is one which has never received from the critics the praise which it undoubtedly deserves:

Though the day of my destiny's over,
   And the star of my fate hath declined,
Thy soft heart refused to discover
   The faults which so many could find;
Though thy soul with my grief was acquainted
   It shrunk not to share it with me,
And the love which my spirit hath painted
   It never hath found but in thee.

Then when nature around me is smiling,
   The last smile which answers to mine,
I do not believe it beguiling,
   Because it reminds me of thine;
And when winds are at war with the ocean,
   As the breasts I believed in with me,

The Poetic Principle

If their billows excite an emotion,
    It is that they bear me from thee.

Though the rock of my last hope is shivered,
    And its fragments are sunk in the wave,
Though I feel that my soul is delivered
    To pain—it shall not be its slave.
There is many a pang to pursue me;
    They may crush, but they shall not contemn;
They may torture, but shall not subdue me;
    'T is of thee that I think—not of them.

Though human, thou didst not deceive me;
    Though woman, thou didst not forsake;
Though loved, thou foreborest to grieve me;
    Though slandered, thou never couldst shake;
Though trusted, thou didst not disclaim me;
    Though parted, it was not to fly;
Though watchful, 't was not to defame me;
    Nor mute, that the world might belie.

Yet I blame not the world, nor despise it,
    Nor the war of the many with one—
If my soul was not fitted to prize it,
    'T was folly not sooner to shun:
And if dearly that error hath cost me,
    And more than I once could foresee,
I have found that whatever it lost me,
    It could not deprive me of thee.

From the wreck of the past, which hath perished,
    Thus much I at least may recall:
It hath taught me that which I most cherished
    Deserved to be dearest of all.

The Poetic Principle

> In the desert a fountain is springing,
>> In the wide waste there still is a tree,
> And a bird in the solitude singing,
>> Which speaks to my spirit of thee.

Although the rhythm here is one of the most difficult the versification could scarcely be improved. No nobler theme ever engaged the pen of poet. It is the soul-elevating idea, that no man can consider himself entitled to complain of fate while, in his adversity, he still retains the unwavering love of woman.

From Alfred Tennyson—although in perfect sincerity I regard him as the noblest poet that ever lived—I have left myself time to cite only a very brief specimen. I call him and think him the noblest of poets, not because the impressions he produces are at all times the most profound; not because the poetical excitement which he induces is at all times the most intense; but because it is at all times the most ethereal, in other words, the most elevating and the most pure. No poet is so little of the earth, earthy. What I am about to read is from his last long poem, *The Princess :*

> Tears, idle tears, I know not what they mean,
> Tears from the depth of some divine despair
> Rise in the heart, and gather to the eyes,
> In looking on the happy autumn-fields,
> And thinking of the days that are no more.

The Poetic Principle

Fresh as the first beam glittering on a sail
That brings our friends up from the underworld,
Sad as the last which reddens over one
That sinks with all we love below the verge;
So sad, so fresh, the days that are no more.

Ah, sad and strange as in dark summer dawns
The earliest pipe of half-awaken'd birds
To dying ears, when unto dying eyes
The casement slowly grows a glimmering square;
So sad, so strange, the days that are no more.

Dear as remember'd kisses after death,
And sweet as those by hopeless fancy feign'd
On lips that are for others; deep as love,
Deep as first love, and wild with all regret;
O Death in Life, the days that are no more.

Thus, although in a very cursory and imperfect manner, I have endeavored to convey to you my conception of the poetic principle. It has been my purpose to suggest that, while this principle itself is, strictly and simply, the human aspiration for supernal beauty, the manifestation of the principle is always found in an elevating excitement of the soul, quite independent of that passion which is the intoxication of the heart, or of that truth which is the satisfaction of the reason. For, in regard to passion, alas! its tendency is to degrade rather than elevate the soul. Love, on the contrary, love, the true, the divine Eros, the Uranian as distinguished from the

The Poetic Principle

Dionæan Venus, is unquestionably the purest and truest of all poetical themes. And in regard to truth, if, to be sure, through the attainment of a truth we are led to perceive a harmony where none was apparent before, we experience at once the true poetical effect; but this effect is referable to the harmony alone and not in the least degree to the truth which merely served to render the harmony manifest.

We shall reach, however, more immediately a distinct conception of what the true poetry is by mere reference to a few of the simple elements which induce in the poet himself the true poetical effect. He recognizes the ambrosia which nourishes his soul in the bright orbs that shine in heaven, in the volutes of the flower, in the clustering of low shrubberies, in the waving of the grain-fields, in the slanting of tall Eastern trees, in the blue distance of mountains, in the grouping of clouds, in the twinkling of half-hidden brooks, in the gleaming of silver rivers, in the repose of sequestered lakes, in the star-mirroring depths of lonely wells. He perceives it in the songs of birds, in the harp of Æolus, in the sighing of the night-wind, in the repining voice of the forest, in the surf that complains to the shore, in the fresh breath of the woods, in the scent of the violet, in the voluptuous perfume of the hyacinth, in the suggestive odor that comes to him at eventide from far-distant, undiscovered islands, over dim oceans illimitable and unexplored. He owns it in

The Poetic Principle

all noble thoughts, in all unworldly motives, in all holy
impulses, in all chivalrous, generous, and self-sacrific-
ing deeds. He feels it in the beauty of woman, in the
grace of her step, in the lustre of her eye, in the melody
of her voice, in the soft laughter, in her sigh, in the
harmony of the rustling of her robes. He deeply feels
it in her winning endearments, in her burning en-
thusiasms, in her gentle charities, in her meek and
devotional endurances; but above all, ah! far above
all he kneels to it, he worships it in the faith, in the
purity, in the strength, in the altogether divine majesty
of her love.

Let me conclude by the recitation of yet another
brief poem, one very different in character from any
that I have before quoted. It is by Motherwell, and
is called *The Song of the Cavalier.* With our modern
and altogether rational ideas of the absurdity and im-
piety of warfare, we are not precisely in that frame of
mind best adapted to sympathize with the sentiments,
and thus to appreciate the real excellence, of the poem.
To do this fully we must identify ourselves, in fancy,
with the soul of the old cavalier.

> Then mounte! then mounte, brave gallants, all,
>   And don your helmes amaine:
> Deathe's couriers, Fame and Honor, call
>   Us to the field againe.
>
> No shrewish teares shall fill our eye
>   When the sword-hilt 's in our hand,—

The Poetic Principle

Heart-whole we 'll part and no whit sighe
  For the fayrest of the land;
Let piping swaine and craven wight,
  Thus weepe and puling crye,
Our business is like men to fight,
  And hero-like to die!

The Rationale of Verse

THE word " verse " is here used not in its strict or primitive sense, but as the term most convenient for expressing generally and without pedantry all that is involved in the consideration of rhythm, rhyme, metre, and versification.

There is, perhaps, no topic in polite literature which has been more pertinaciously discussed, and there is certainly not one about which so much inaccuracy, confusion, misconception, misrepresentation, mystification, and downright ignorance on all sides can be fairly said to exist. Were the topic really difficult, or did it lie even in the cloud-land of metaphysics, where the doubt-vapors may be made to assume any and every shape at the will or at the fancy of the gazer, we should have less reason to wonder at all this contradiction and perplexity; but in fact the subject is exceedingly simple: one tenth of it, possibly, may be called ethical; nine tenths, however, appertain to mathematics; and the whole is included within the limits of the commonest common sense.

"But, if this is the case, how," it will be asked, "can so much misunderstanding have arisen? Is it conceivable that a thousand profound scholars, investigating so very simple a matter for centuries, have not been able to place it in the fullest light, at least, of which it is susceptible?" These queries, I confess, are not easily answered; at all events a satisfactory reply to them might cost more trouble than would if properly considered, the whole *vexata quæstío* to which they have reference. Nevertheless, there is little difficulty or danger in suggesting that the "thousand profound scholars" may have failed, first, because they were scholars; secondly, because they were profound; and, thirdly, because they were a thousand, the impotency of the scholarship and profundity having been thus multiplied a thousandfold. I am serious in these suggestions; for, first again, there is something in "scholarship" which seduces us into blind worship of Bacon's Idol of the Theatre, into irrational deference to antiquity; secondly, the proper "profundity" is rarely profound—it is the nature of truth in general, as of some ores in particular, to be richest when most superficial; thirdly, the clearest subject may be overclouded by mere superabundance of talk. In chemistry the best way of separating two bodies is to add a third; in speculation, fact often agrees with fact and argument with argument, until an additional well-meaning fact or argument sets everything by the ears. In one case out of a hundred a point is excessively discussed because it is obscure; in the ninety-nine remaining it is obscure because excessively discussed. When a topic is thus circumstanced, the readiest mode of investigating it is to forget that any previous investigation has been attempted.

But, in fact, while much has been written on the Greek and Latin rhythms, and even on the Hebrew, little effort has been made at examining that of any of the modern tongues. As regards the English, comparatively nothing has been done. It may be said, indeed, that we are without a treatise on our own verse. In our ordinary grammars and in our works on rhetoric or prosody in general, may be found occasional chapters, it is true, which have the heading " Versification," but these are, in all instances, exceedingly meagre. They pretend to no analysis; they propose nothing like system; they make no attempt at even rule; every thing depends upon " authority." They are confined, in fact, to mere exemplification of the supposed varieties of English feet and English lines; although in no work with which I am acquainted are these feet correctly given or these lines detailed in anything like their full extent. Yet what has been mentioned is all, if we except the occasional introduction of some pedagogism, such as this, borrowed from the Greek prosodies: " When a syllable is wanting, the verse is said to be catalectic; when the measure is exact, the line is acatalectic; when there is a redundant syllable it forms hypermeter." Now whether a line be termed catalectic or acatalectic is, perhaps, a point of no vital importance; it is even possible that the student may be able to decide promptly, when the a should be employed and when omitted, yet be incognizant, at the same time, of all that is worth knowing in regard to the structure of verse.

A leading defect in each of our treatises, if treatises they can be called, is the confining the subject to mere versification while verse in general, with the understanding given to the term in the heading of this paper, is the real question at issue. Nor am I aware of even one of our grammars which so much as properly defines the word " versification " itself. " Versification," says a work now before me, of which the accuracy is far more than usual,—the *English Grammar* of Goold Brown,—" Versification is the art of arranging words into lines of correspondent length, so as to produce harmony by the regular alternation of syllables differing in quantity." The commencement of this definition might apply, indeed, to the art of versification, but not versification itself. Versification is not the art of arranging, etc., but the actual arranging—a distinction too obvious to need comment. The error here is identical with one which has been too long permitted to disgrace the initial page of every one of our school grammars. I allude to the definitions of English grammar itself. " English grammar," it is said, " is the art of speaking and writing the English language correctly." This phraseology, or something essentially similar, is employed, I believe, by Bacon, Miller, Fisk, Greenleaf, Ingersoll, Kirkland, Cooper, Flint, Pue, Comly, and many others. These gentlemen, it is presumed, adopted it, without examination, from Murray, who derived it from Lily (whose work was *quam solam Regia Majestas in omnibus scholis docendam præ-cipit),* and who appropriated it without acknowledgment, but with some unimportant modification, from the Latin grammar of Leonicenus. It may be shown, however, that this definition, so complacently received, is not, and cannot be, a proper definition of English grammar. A definition is that which so describes its object as to distinguish it from all others; it is no definition of any one thing if its terms are applicable to any one other. But if it be asked " What is the design, the end, the aim of English grammar? " our obvious answer is: " The art of speaking and writing the English language correctly "; that is to say, we must use the precise words employed as the definition of English grammar itself.

The Rationale of Verse

But the object to be attained by any means is, assuredly, not the means. English grammar and the end contemplated by English grammar are two matters sufficiently distinct; nor can the one be more reasonably regarded as the other than a fishing-hook as a fish. The definition, therefore, which is applicable in the latter instance, cannot, in the former, be true. Grammar in general is the analysis of language; English grammar, of the English.

But to return to versification as defined in our extract above. "It is the art," says the extract, " of arranging words into lines of correspondent length." Not so: a correspondence in the length of lines is by no means essential. Pindaric odes are, surely, instances of versification, yet these compositions are noted for extreme diversity in the length of their lines.

The arrangement is, moreover, said to be for the purpose of producing " harmony by the regular alternation," etc. But harmony is not the sole aim; not even the principal one. In the construction of verse, melody should never be left out of view; yet this is a point which all our prosodies have most unaccountably forborne to touch. Reasoned rules on this topic should form a portion of all systems of rhythm.

" So as to produce harmony," says the definition, " by the regular alternation," etc. A regular alternation, as described, forms no part of any principle of versification. The arrangement of spondees and dactyls, for example, in the Greek hexameter, is an arrangement which may be termed "at random." At least it is arbitrary. Without interference with the line as a whole, a dactyl may be substituted for a spondee, or the converse, at any point other than the ultimate and penultimate feet, of which the former is always a spondee, the latter nearly always a dactyl. Here, it is clear, we have no " regular alternation of syllables differing in quantity."

" So as to produce harmony," proceeds the definition, " by the regular alternation of syllables differing in quantity,"—in other words, by the alternation of long and short syllables; for in rhythm all syllables are necessarily either short or long. But not only do I deny the necessity of any regularity in the succession of feet and, by consequence, of syllables, but dispute the essentiality of any alternation, regular or irregular, of syllables long and short. Our author, observe, is now engaged in a definition of versification in general, not of English versification in particular. But the Greek and Latin metres abound in the spondee and pyrrhic, the former consisting of two long syllables, the latter of two short; and there are innumerable instances of the immediate succession of many spondees and many pyrrhics.

Here is a passage from Silius Italicus:

The Rationale of Verse

Fallis te mensas inter quod credis inermem
Tot bellis quæsita viro, tot cædibus armat
Majestas æterna ducem : si admoveris ora
Cannas et Trebium ante oculos Trasymenaque busta,
Et Pauli stare ingentem miraberis umbram.

Making the elisions demanded by the classic prosodies, we should scan these hexameters thus:

Fāllĭs | tē mēn | sās ĭn | tēr qŭod | crēdĭs ĭn | ērmēm |
Tŏt bēl | lĭs qūæ | sītă vĭ | rō tŏt | cædĭbŭs | ārmāt |
Mājēs | tās ǣ | tērnă dŭ | cēm s'ād | mōvĕrĭs | ōrā |
Cānnās | ĕt Trĕbĭ' | ānt'ŏcŭ | lōs Trăsy̆ | mēnăqŭe | būstă |
Ēt Pāu | lī stā | r'īngēn | tēm mī | rābĕrĭs | ūmbrām. |

It will be seen that, in the first and last of these lines, we have only two short syllables in thirteen, with an uninterrupted succession of no less than nine long syllables. But how are we to reconcile all this with a definition of versification which describes it as " the art of arranging words into lines of correspondent length so as to produce harmony by the regular alternation of syllables differing in quantity " ?

It may be urged, however, that our prosodist's intention was to speak of the English metres alone, and that, by omitting all mention of the spondee and pyrrhic, he has virtually avowed their exclusion from our rhythms. A grammarian is never excusable on the ground of good intentions. We demand from him, if from any one, rigorous precision of style. But grant the design. Let us admit that our author, following the example of all authors on English prosody, has, in defining versification at large, intended a definition merely of the English. All these prosodists, we will say, reject the spondee and pyrrhic. Still all admit the iambus, which consists of a short syllable followed by a long; the trochee, which is the converse of the iambus; the dactyl, formed of one long syllable followed by two short; and the anapæst, two short succeeded by a long. The spondee is improperly rejected, as I shall presently show. The pyrrhic is rightfully dismissed. Its existence in either ancient or modern rhythm is purely chimerical, and the insisting on so perplexing a nonentity as a foot of two short syllables affords, perhaps, the best evidence of the gross irrationality and subservience to authority which characterize our prosody. In the meantime the acknowledged dactyl and anapæst are enough to sustain my proposition about the " alternation," etc., without reference to feet which are assumed to exist in the Greek and Latin metres alone: for an anapæst and a dactyl may meet in the same line; when, of course, we shall have an uninterrupted succession of four short syllables. The meeting of these two feet, to be sure, is an accident not contemplated in the definition now discussed; for this definition, in demanding a " regular alternation of syllables differing in quantity," insists on a regular succession of similar feet. But here is an example:

The Rationale of Verse

Sĭng tŏ mĕ | Ĭsăbĕlle.

This is the opening line of a little ballad now before me, which proceeds in the same rhythm, a peculiarly beautiful one. More than all this: English lines are often well composed entirely of a regular succession of syllables all of the same quantity; the first lines, for instance, of the following quatrain by Arthur C. Coxe:

> *March ! march ! march !*
>   Making sounds as they tread.
> Ho! ho! how they step,
>   Going down to the dead!

The line italicized is formed of three cæsuras. The cæsura, of which I have much to say hereafter, is rejected by the English prosodies and grossly misrepresented in the classic. It is a perfect foot, the most important in all verse, and consists of a single long syllable; but the length of this syllable varies.

It has thus been made evident that there is not one point of the definition in question which does not involve an error. And for anything more satisfactory or more intelligible we shall look in vain to any published treatise on the topic.

So general and so total a failure can be referred only to radical misconception. In fact, the English prosodists have blindly followed the pedants. These latter, like *les moutons de Panurge,* have been occupied in incessant tumbling into ditches, for the excellent reason that their leaders have so tumbled before. The *Iliad*, being taken as a starting-point, was made to stand instead of nature and common sense. Upon this poem, in place of facts and deduction from fact, or from natural law, were built systems of feet, metres, rhythms, rules,—rules that contradict each other every five minutes, and for nearly all of which there may be found twice as many exceptions as examples. If any one has a fancy to be thoroughly confounded, to see how far the infatuation of what is termed " classical scholarship " can lead a bookworm in the manufacture of darkness out of sunshine, let him turn over for a few moments any of the German Greek prosodies. The only thing clearly made out in them is a very magnificent contempt for Leibnitz's principle of " a sufficient reason."

To divert attention from the real matter in hand by any further reference to these works is unnecessary and would be weak. I cannot call to mind at this moment one essential particular of information that is to be gleaned from them; and I will drop them here with merely this one observation: that, employing from among the numerous " ancient " feet the spondee, the trochee, the iambus, the anapæst, the dactyl, and the cæsura alone, I will engage to scan correctly any of the Horatian rhythms, or any true rhythm that human ingenuity can conceive. And this excess of chimerical feet is, perhaps, the very least of the scholastic supererogations. *Ex uno disce omnia,* The fact is, that quantity is a point in whose investigation the lumber of mere learning may be dispensed with, if ever in any. Its appreciation is universal. It appertains to no region, nor race, nor era in especial. To melody and to harmony the Greeks hearkened with ears precisely similar to those which we employ for similar purposes at present; and I should not be condemned for heresy in asserting that a pendulum at Athens would have vibrated much after the same fashion as does a pendulum in the city of Penn.

Verse originates in the human enjoyment of equality, fitness. To this enjoyment, also, all the moods of verse—rhythm, metre, stanza, rhyme, alliteration, the refrain, and other analogous effects—are to be referred. As there are some readers who habitually confound rhythm and metre, it may be as well here to say that the former concerns the character of feet (that is, the arrangement of syllables), while the latter has to do with the number of these feet. Thus, by " a dactylic rhythm " we express a sequence of dactyls. By " a dactylic hexameter " we imply a line or measure consisting of six of these dactyls.

To return to equality. Its idea embraces those of similarity, proportion, identity, repetition, and adaptation or fitness. It might not be very difficult to go even behind the idea of equality, and show both how and why it is that the human nature takes pleasure in

The Rationale of Verse

it, but such an investigation would, for any purpose now in view, be supererogatory. It is sufficient that the fact is undeniable—the fact that man derives enjoyment from his perception of equality. Let us examine a crystal. We are at once interested by the equality between the sides and between the angles of one of its faces: the equality of the sides pleases us; that of the angles doubles the pleasure. On bringing to view a second face in all respects similar to the first, this pleasure seems to be squared; on bringing to view a third it appears to be cubed, and so on. I have no doubt, indeed, that the delight experienced, if measurable, would be found to have exact mathematical relations such as I suggest; that is to say, as far as a certain point, beyond which there would be a decrease in similar relations.

The perception of pleasure in the equality of sounds is the principle of music. Unpractised ears can appreciate only simple equalities, such as are found in ballad airs. While comparing one simple sound with another they are too much occupied to be capable of comparing the equality subsisting between these two simple sounds, taken conjointly, and two other similar simple sounds taken conjointly. Practised ears, on the other hand, appreciate both equalities at the same instant, although it is absurd to suppose that both are heard at the same instant. One is heard and appreciated from itself; the other is heard by the memory;

The Rationale of Verse

and the instant glides into and is confounded with the secondary appreciation. Highly cultivated musical taste in this manner enjoys not only these double equalities, all appreciated at once, but takes pleasurable cognizance, through memory, of equalities the members of which occur at intervals so great that the uncultivated taste loses them altogether. That this latter can properly estimate or decide on the merits of what is called scientific music is, of course, impossible. But scientific music has no claim to intrinsic excellence, it is fit for scientific ears alone. In its excess it is the triumph of the *physique* over the *morale* of music. The sentiment is overwhelmed by the sense. On the whole, the advocates of the simpler melody and harmony have infinitely the best of the argument, although there has been very little of real argument on the subject.

In verse, which cannot be better designated than as an inferior or less capable music, there is, happily, little chance for perplexity. Its rigidly simple character not even science, not even pedantry can greatly pervert.

The rudiment of verse may possibly be found in the spondee. The very germ of a thought seeking satisfaction in equality of sound would result in the construction of words of two syllables equally accented. In corroboration of this idea we find that spondees most abound in the most ancient tongues. The second

step we can easily suppose to be the comparison, that
is to say, the collocation, of two spondees—of two
words composed each of a spondee. The third step
would be the juxtaposition of three of these words.
By this time the perception of monotone would induce
further consideration: and thus arises what Leigh
Hunt so flounders in discussing under the title of " The
Principle of Variety in Uniformity." Of course there
is no principle in the case, nor in maintaining it. The
" uniformity " is the principle; the " variety " is but
the principle's natural safeguard from self-destruction
by excess of self. " Uniformity," besides, is the very
worst word that could have been chosen for the ex-
pression of the general idea at which it aims.

The perception of monotone having given rise to an
attempt at its relief, the first thought in this new direc-
tion would be that of collating two or more words
formed each of two syllables differently accented (that
is to say, short and long) but having the same order in
each word,—in other terms, of collating two or more
iambuses or two or more trochees. And here let me
pause to assert that more pitiable nonsense has been
written on the topic of long and short syllables than on
any other subject under the sun. In general, a syl-
lable is long or short, just as it is difficult or easy of
enunciation. The natural long syllables are those en-
cumbered, the natural short syllables are those unen-
cumbered, with consonants; all the rest is mere

The Rationale of Verse

artificiality and jargon. The Latin prosodies have a rule that " a vowel before two consonants is long." This rule is deduced from " authority," that is, from the observation that vowels so circumstanced in the ancient poems are always in syllables long by the laws of scansion. The philosophy of the rule is untouched, and lies simply in the physical difficulty of giving voice to such syllables—of performing the lingual evolutions necessary for their utterance. Of course, it is not the vowel that is long (although the rule says so), but the syllable of which the vowel is a part. It will be seen that the length of a syllable, depending on the facility or difficulty of its enunciation, must have great variation in various syllables; but for the purposes of verse we suppose a long syllable equal to two short ones; and the natural deviation from this relativeness we correct in perusal. The more closely our long syllables approach this relation with our short ones, the better, *ceteris paribus,* will be our verse; but if the relation does not exist of itself we force it by emphasis, which can, of course, make any syllable as long as desired; or, by an effort we can pronounce with unnatural brevity a syllable that is naturally too long. Accented syllables are, of course, always long, but, where unencumbered with consonants, must be classed among the unnaturally long. Mere custom has declared that we shall accent them, that is to say, dwell upon them; but no inevitable lingual difficulty forces us to do so. In a line, every long syllable must of its own accord occupy in its utterance, or must be made to occupy, precisely the time demanded for two short ones. The only exception to this rule is found in the cæsura, of which more anon.

The success of the experiment with the trochees or iambuses (the one would have suggested the other) must have led to a trial of dactyls or anapæsts, natural dactyls or anapæsts, dactylic or anapæstic words. And now some degree of complexity has been attained. There is an appreciation, first, of the equality between the several dactyls or anapæsts, and, secondly, of that between the long syllable and the two short conjointly. But here it may be said that step after step would have been taken, in continuation of this routine, until all the feet of the Greek prosodies became exhausted. Not so: these remaining feet have no existence except in the brains of the scholiasts. It is needless to imagine men inventing these things, and folly to explain how and why they invented them, until it shall be first shown that they are actually invented. All other " feet " than those which I have specified are, if not impossible at first view, merely combinations of the specified; and, although this assertion is rigidly true, I will, to avoid misunderstanding, put it in a somewhat different shape. I will say, then, that at present I am aware of no rhythm—nor do I believe that any one can be constructed—which, in its last analysis, will not be found to consist altogether of the feet I have mentioned, either existing in their individual and obvious condition, or interwoven with each other in accordance with simple natural laws which I will endeavor to point out hereafter.

We have now gone so far as to suppose men constructing indefinite sequences of spondaic, iambic, trochaic, dactylic, or anapæstic words. In extending these sequences, they would be again arrested by the sense of monotone. A succession of spondees would immediately have displeased; one of iambuses or of trochees, on account of the variety included within the foot itself, would have taken longer to displease; one of dactyls or anapæsts, still longer; but even the last, if extended very far, must have become wearisome. The idea, first, of curtailing, and, secondly, of defining the length of a sequence, would thus at once have arisen. Here, then, is the line, or verse proper.[1] The principle of equality being constantly at the bottom of the whole process, lines would naturally be made, in the first instance, equal in the number of their feet; in the second instance, there would be variation in the mere number: one line would be twice as long as

---

[1] Verse, from the Latin *vertere* (to turn) is so called on account of the turning or recommencement of the series of feet. Thus a verse, strictly speaking, is a line. In this sense, however, I have preferred using the latter word alone; employing the former in the general acceptation given it in the heading of this paper.

another; then one would be some less obvious multiple of another; then still less obvious proportions would be adopted; nevertheless there would be proportion, that is to say, a phase of equality, still.

Lines being once introduced, the necessity of distinctly defining these lines to the ear (as yet, written verse does not exist) would lead to a scrutiny of their capabilities at their terminations; and now would spring up the idea of equality in sound between the final syllables—in other words, of rhyme. First, it would be used only in the iambic, anapæstic, and spondaic rhythms (granting that the latter had not been thrown aside long since on account of its tameness), because in these rhythms the concluding syllable, being long, could best sustain the necessary protraction of the voice. No great while could elapse, however, before the effect, found pleasant as well as useful, would be applied to the two remaining rhythms. But as the chief force of rhyme must lie in the accented syllable, the attempt to create rhyme at all in these two remaining rhythms, the trochaic and dactylic, would necessarily result in double and triple rhymes, such as "beauty" with "duty" (trochaic) and "beautiful" with "dutiful" (dactylic).

It must be observed that in suggesting these processes I assign them no date; nor do I even insist upon their order. Rhyme is supposed to be of modern origin, and were this proved, my positions remain untouched. I may say, however, in passing, that several instances of rhyme occur in the *Clouds* of Aristophanes, and that the Roman poets occasionally employ it. There is an effective species of ancient rhyming which has never descended to the moderns: that in which the ultimate and penultimate syllables rhyme with each other. For example:

Parturiunt montes et nascitur ridicu*lus mus,*

And again:

Litoreis ingens inventa sub ilici*bus sus,*

The terminations of Hebrew verse, as far as understood, show no signs of rhyme; but what thinking person can doubt that it did actually exist? That men have so obstinately and blindly insisted, in general, even up to the present day, in confining rhyme to the ends of lines when its effect is even better applicable elsewhere, intimates, in my opinion, the sense of some necessity in the connection of the end with the rhyme, hints that the origin of rhyme lay in a necessity which connected it with the end, shows that neither mere accident nor mere fancy gave rise to the connection, points, in a word, at the very necessity which I have suggested (that of some mode of defining lines to the ear) as the true origin of rhyme. Admit this, and we throw the origin far back in the night of time, beyond the origin of written verse.

But to resume. The amount of complexity I have

now supposed to be attained is very considerable. Various systems of equalization are appreciated at once, or nearly so, in their respective values and in the value of each system with reference to all the others. As our present ultimatum of complexity we have arrived at triple-rhymed, natural-dactylic lines, existing proportionally, as well as equally, with regard to other triple-rhymed, natural-dactylic lines. For example:

> Virginal Lilian, rigidly, humblily dutiful;
> Saintlily, lowlily,
> Thrillingly, holily
> Beautiful!

Here we appreciate, first, the absolute equality between the long syllable of each dactyl and the two short conjointly; secondly, the absolute equality between each dactyl and any other dactyl—in other words, among all the dactyls; thirdly, the absolute equality between the two middle lines; fourthly, the absolute equality between the first line and the three others taken conjointly; fifthly, the absolute equality between the last two syllables of the respective words " dutiful " and " beautiful " ; sixthly, the absolute equality between the last two syllables of the respective words " lowlily " and " holily "; seventhly, the proximate equality between the first syllable of " dutiful " and the first syllable of " beautiful " ; eighthly, the proximate equality between the first syllable of

" lowlily " and that of " holily " ; ninthly, the proportional equality (that of five to one) between the first line and each of its members, the dactyls; tenthly, the proportional equality (that of two to one) between each of the middle lines and its members, the dactyls; eleventhly, the proportional equality between the first line and each of the two middle—that of five to two; twelfthly, the proportional equality between the first line and the last—that of five to one; thirteenthly, the proportional equality between each of the middle lines and the last—that of two to one; lastly, the proportional equality as concerns number between all the lines taken collectively and any individual line—that of four to one.

The consideration of this last equality would give birth immediately to the idea of stanza [1]; that is to say, the insulation of lines into equal or obviously proportional masses. In its primitive (which was also its best) form, the stanza would most probably have had absolute unity. In other words, the removal of any one of its lines would have rendered it imperfect; as in the case above, where, if the last line, for example, be taken away, there is left no rhyme to the " dutiful " of the first. Modern stanza is excessively loose, and, where so, ineffective, as a matter of course.

Now, although in the deliberate written statement which I have here given of these various systems of

---

[1] A stanza is often vulgarly, and with gross impropriety, called a verse.

The Rationale of Verse

equalities, there seems to be an infinity of complexity,
—so much that it is hard to conceive the mind taking
cognizance of them all in the brief period occupied by
the perusal or recital of the stanza; yet the difficulty
is, in fact, apparent only when we will it to become so.
Any one fond of mental experiment may satisfy him-
self by trial that, in listening to the lines, he does
actually, although with a seeming unconsciousness on
account of the rapid evolutions of sensation, recognize
and instantaneously appreciate, more or less intensely
as his ear is cultivated, each and all of the equaliza-
tions detailed. The pleasure received, or receivable,
has very much such progressive increase, and in very
nearly such mathematical relations as those which I
have suggested in the case of the crystal.

It will be observed that I speak of merely a proxi-
mate equality between the first syllable of " dutiful "
and that of " beautiful "; and it may be asked why
we cannot imagine the earliest rhymes to have had
absolute instead of proximate equality of sound. But
absolute equality would have involved the use of iden-
tical words; and it is the duplicate sameness or monot-
ony—that of sense as well as that of sound—which
would have caused these rhymes to be rejected in the
very first instance.

The narrowness of the limits within which verse
composed of natural feet alone must necessarily have
been confined, would have led, after a very brief inter-

The Rationale of Verse

val, to the trial and immediate adoption of artificial feet; that is to say, of feet not constituted each of a single word, but two or even three words, or of parts of words. These feet would be intermingled with natural ones. For example:

Ă brēath | căn māke | thĕm ās | ă brēath | hăs māde. .

This is an iambic line in which each iambus is formed of two words. Again:

Thĕ ūn | ĭmā | gĭnā | blĕ mīght | ŏf Jŏve.

This is an iambic line in which the first foot is formed of a word and a part of a word; the second and third, of parts taken from the body or interior of a word; the fourth, of a part and a whole; the fifth, of two complete words. There are no natural feet in either lines. Again:

Căn ĭt bĕ | fănciĕd thăt | Dēĭty | ĕvĕr vĭn | dīctĭvely
Māde ĭn hĭs | īmăge ă | mānnĭkĭn | mĕrely tŏ | māddĕn ĭt ?

These are two dactylic lines in which we find natural feet (" Deity," " mannikin "), feet composed of two words (" fancied that," " image a," " merely to," " madden it "), feet composed of three words (" can it be," " made in his "), a foot composed of a part of a word (" dictively "), and a foot composed of a word and a part of a word (" ever vin ").

And now, in our supposititious progress, we have gone so far as to exhaust all the essentialities of verse.

The Rationale of Verse

What follows may, strictly speaking, be regarded as
embellishment merely, but even in this embellishment
the rudimental sense of equality would have been the
never-ceasing impulse. It would, for example, be
simply in seeking further administration to this sense
that men would come, in time, to think of the refrain,
or burden, where, at the closes of the several stanzas
of a poem, one word or phrase is repeated; and of
alliteration, in whose simplest form a consonant is
repeated in the commencements of various words.
This effect would be extended so as to embrace repeti-
tions both of vowels and of consonants in the bodies as
well as in the beginnings of words; and, at a later
period, would be made to infringe on the province of
rhyme by the introduction of general similarity of
sound between whole feet occurring in the body of a
line—all of which modifications I have exemplified in
the line above,

Made in his image a *mannikin* merely to *madden it.*

Farther cultivation would improve also the refrain by
relieving its monotone in slightly varying the phrase
at each repetition, or, as I have attempted to do in
The Raven, in retaining the phrase and varying its
application; although this latter point is not strictly a
rhythmical effect alone. Finally, poets when fairly
wearied with following precedent—following it the
more closely the less they perceived it in company with

The Rationale of Verse

reason—would adventure so far as to indulge in positive rhyme at other points than the ends of lines. First, they would put it in the middle of the line; then at some point where the multiple would be less obvious; then, alarmed at their own audacity, they would undo all their work by cutting these lines in two. And here is the fruitful source of the infinity of " short metre," by which modern poetry, if not distinguished, is at least disgraced. It would require a high degree, indeed, both of cultivation and of courage, on the part of any versifier, to enable him to place his rhymes, and let them remain, at unquestionably their best position, that of unusual and unanticipated intervals.

On account of the stupidity of some people, or, if talent be a more respectable word, on account of their talent for misconception, I think it necessary to add here, first, that I believe the " processes " above detailed to be nearly if not accurately those which did occur in the gradual creation of what we now call verse; secondly, that, although I so believe, I yet urge neither the assumed fact nor my belief in it as a part of the true propositions of this paper; thirdly, that in regard to the aim of this paper it is of no consequence whether these processes did occur either in the order I have assigned them, or at all; my design being simply, in presenting a general type of what such processes might have been and must have resembled, to

help them, the " some people," to an easy understand-
ing of what I have further to say on the topic of Verse.

There is one point which, in my summary of the
processes, I have purposely forborne to touch; because
this point, being the most important of all, on account
of the immensity of error usually involved in its con-
sideration, would have led me into a series of detail
inconsistent with the object of a summary.

Every reader of verse must have observed how sel-
dom it happens that even any one line proceeds uni-
formly with a succession, such as I have supposed, of
absolutely equal feet; that is to say, with a succession
of iambuses only, or of trochees only, or of· dactyls
only, or of anapæsts only, or of spondees only. Even
in the most musical lines we find the succession in-
terrupted. The iambic pentameters of Pope, for ex-
ample, will be found, on examination, frequently varied
by trochees in the beginning, or by, what seem to be,
anapæsts in the body, of the line.

> Ŏh thoū | whătē | vĕr tī | tlĕ plēase | thĭne ēar
> Dĕan Drā | pĭĕr Bīck | ĕrstāff | ŏr Gūl | ĭvĕr
> Whēthĕr | thŏu choōse | Cĕrvān | tĕs' sē | rĭoŭs aīr
> Ŏr laūgh | ănd shāke | ĭn Rāb | ĕlăis' ēa | sy chāir.

Were any one weak enough to refer to the prosodies
for the solution of the difficulty here, he would find it
solved, as usual, by a rule, stating the fact, or what it,
the rule, supposes to be the fact, but without the
slightest attempt at the rationale. " By a synæresis of

the two short syllables," say the books, " an anapæst may sometimes be employed for an iambus, or a dactyl for a trochee. . . . In the beginning of a line a trochee is often used for an iambus."

" Blending " is the plain English for " synæresis," but there should be no blending; neither is an anapæst ever employed for an iambus, or a dactyl for a trochee. These feet differ in time; and no feet so differing can ever be legitimately used in the same line. An anapæst is equal to four short syllables, an iambus only to three. Dactyls and trochees hold the same relation. The principle of equality in verse admits, it is true, of variation at certain points for the relief of monotone, as I have already shown, but the point of time is that point which, being the rudimental one, must never be tampered with at all.

To explain:—In further efforts for the relief of monotone than those to which I have alluded in the summary, men soon came to see that there was no absolute necessity for adhering to the precise number of syllables, provided the time required for the whole foot was preserved inviolate. They saw, for instance, that in such a line as

Ŏr laūgh | ănd shāke | ĭn Rāb | ĕlăis' ēa | sy chāir,

the equalization of the three syllables " elais' ea " with the two syllables composing any of the other feet, could be readily effected by pronouncing the two syl-

lables " elais' " in double-quick time. By pronouncing
each of the syllables " e " and " lais' " twice as rapidly
as the syllable " sy," or the syllable " in," or any other
syllable, they could bring the two of them, taken to-
gether, to the length, that is to say, to the time, of any
one short syllable. This consideration enabled them
to effect the agreeable variation of three syllables in
place of the uniform two. And variation was the object
—variation to the ear. What sense is there, then, in
supposing this object rendered null by the blending of
the two syllables so as to render them, in absolute
effect, one ? Of course, there must be no blending.
Each syllable must be pronounced as distinctly as pos-
sible, or the variation is lost, but with twice the rapid-
ity in which the ordinary syllable is enunciated. That
the syllables "elais' ea" do not compose an anapæst is
evident, and the signs (ăăā) of their accentuation are
erroneous. The foot might be written thus : " ȃȃā," the
inverted crescents expressing double-quick time; and
might be called a bastard iambus.

Here is a trochaic line:

Sēe thĕ | dēlĭcăte | fōotĕd | rēindeĕr.

The prosodies—that is to say, the most considerate of
them—would here decide that " delicate " is a dactyl
used in place of a trochee, and would refer to what
they call their " rule," for justification. Others,
varying the stupidity, would insist upon a Procrustean

The Rationale of Verse

adjustment thus: " del'cate "—an adjustment recommended to all such words as " silvery," " murmuring," etc., which, it is said, should be not only pronounced but written " silv'ry," " murm'ring," and so on, whenever they find themselves in trochaic predicament. I have only to say that " delicate," when circumstanced as above, is neither a dactyl nor a dactyl's equivalent; that I would suggest for it this (āăă) accentuation; that I think it as well to call it a bastard trochee; and that all words, at all events, should be written and pronounced in full, and as nearly as possible as nature intended them.

About eleven years ago, there appeared in the *American Monthly Magazine* (then edited, I believe, by Messrs. Hoffman and Benjamin) a review of Mr. Willis's *Poems;* the critic putting forth his strength or his weakness in an endeavor to show that the poet was either absurdly affected or grossly ignorant of the laws of verse; the accusation being based altogether on the fact that Mr. W. made occasional use of this very word " delicate," and other similar words, in " the heroic measure, which every one knew consisted of feet of two syllables." Mr. W. has often, for example, such lines as

" That binds him to a woman's *delicate* love."
" In the gay sunshine, *reverent* in the storm."
" With its *invisible* fingers my loose hair."

The Rationale of Verse

Here, of course, the feet " licate love," " verent in," and " sible fin " are bastard iambuses; are not anapæsts; and are not improperly used. Their employment, on the contrary, by Mr. Willis, is but one of the innumerable instances he has given of keen sensibility in all those matters of taste which may be classed under the general head of " fanciful embellishment."

It is also about eleven years ago, if I am not mistaken, since Mr. Horne, of England, the author of *Orion,* one of the noblest epics in any language, thought it necessary to preface his *Chaucer Modernized* by a very long and evidently a very elaborate essay, of which the greater portion was occupied in a discussion of the seemingly anomalous foot of which we have been speaking. Mr. Horne upholds Chaucer in its frequent use; maintains his superiority, on account of his so frequently using it, over all English versifiers; and, indignantly repelling the common idea of those who make verse on their fingers, that the superfluous syllable is a roughness and an error, very chivalrously makes battle for it as " a grace." That a grace it is, there can be no doubt; and what I complain of is that the author of the most happily versified long poem in existence should have been under the necessity of discussing this grace merely as a grace, through forty or fifty vague pages, solely because of his inability to show how and why it is a grace—by which showing the question would have been settled in an instant.

The Rationale of Verse

About the trochee used for an iambus, as we see in the beginning of the line,

Whēthĕr thou choose Cervantes' serious air,

there is little that need be said. It brings me to the general proposition that in all rhythms the prevalent or distinctive feet may be varied at will, and nearly at random, by the occasional introduction of equivalent feet; that is to say, feet the sum of whose syllabic times is equal to the sum of the syllabic times of the distinctive feet. Thus the trochee " whēthĕr " is equal, in the sum of the times of its syllables, to the iambus " thoŭ chōose " in the sum of the times of its syllables, each foot being, in time, equal to three short syllables. Good versifiers, who happen to be, also, good poets, contrive to relieve the monotone of a series of feet by the use of equivalent feet only at rare intervals, and at such points of their subject as seem in accordance with the startling character of the variation. Nothing of this care is seen in the line quoted above, although Pope has some fine instances of the duplicate effect. Where vehemence is to be strongly expressed I am not sure that we should be wrong in venturing on two consecutive equivalent feet, although I cannot say that I have ever known the adventure made, except in the following passage, which occurs in *Al Aaraaf,* a boyish poem, written by myself when a boy. I am referring to the sudden and rapid advent of a star:

The Rationale of Verse

Dim was its little disk, and angel eyes
Alone could see the phantom in the skies,
Whĕn fīrst thĕ phāntŏm's cōurse wăs foūnd tŏ bĕ
*Hĕadlŏng hĭthĕr*ward o'er the starry sea.

In the " general proposition " above I speak of the occasional introduction of equivalent feet. It sometimes happens that unskilful versifiers, without knowing what they do, or why they do it, introduce so many variations as to exceed in number the distinctive feet; when the ear becomes at once balked by the *bouleversement* of the rhythm. Too many trochees, for example, inserted in an iambic rhythm, would convert the latter to a trochaic. I may note here that, in all cases, the rhythm designed should be commenced and continued, without variation, until the ear has had full time to comprehend what is the rhythm. In violation of a rule so obviously founded in common sense, many even of our best poets do not scruple to begin an iambic rhythm with a trochee, or the converse; or a dactylic with an anapæst, or the converse; and so on.

A somewhat less objectionable error, although still a decided one, is that of commencing a rhythm, not with a different equivalent foot, but with a bastard foot of the rhythm intended. For example:

Māny ă | thōught wĭll | cōme tŏ | mĕmŏry.

Here " many a " is what I have explained to be a bastard trochee, and to be understood should be accented with inverted crescents. It is objectionable solely on account of its position as the opening foot of a trochaic rhythm. " Memory " similarly accented, is also a bastard trochee, but unobjectionable, although by no means demanded.

The further illustration of this point will enable me to take an important step.

One of the finest poets, Mr. Christopher Pearse Cranch, begins a very beautiful poem thus:

> Many are the thoughts that come to me
> In my lonely musing;
> And they drift so strange and swift
> There 's no time for choosing
> Which to follow; for to leave
> Any, seems a losing.

"A losing " to Mr. Cranch, of course—but this *en passant.* It will be seen here that the intention is trochaic, although we do not see this intention by the opening foot, as we should do, or even by the opening line. Reading the whole stanza, however, we perceive the trochaic rhythm as the general design, and so, after some reflection, we divide the first line thus:

Many are the | thŏughts thăt | cŏme tŏ | mē.

Thus scanned, the line will seem musical. It is—highly so. And it is because there is no end to instances of just such lines of apparently incomprehensible music, that Coleridge thought proper to invent his nonsensical system of what he calls " scanning by

accents "—as if " scanning by accents " were any-
thing more than a phrase. Wherever *Christabel* is
really not rough, it can be as readily scanned by the
true laws, not the supposititious rules, of verse as can
the simplest pentameter of Pope; and where it is
rough (*passim*), these same laws will enable any one of
common sense to show why it is rough, and to point
out instantaneously the remedy for the roughness.

A reads and re-reads a certain line and pronounces it
false in rhythm, unmusical. *B,* however, reads it to
A, and *A* is at once struck with the perfection of the
rhythm and wonders at his dulness in not " catching "
it before. Henceforward he admits the line to be
musical. *B,* triumphant, asserts that, to be sure, the
line is musical,—for it is the work of Coleridge,—and
that it is *A* who is not; the fault being in *A's* false
reading. Now here *A* is right and *B* wrong. That
rhythm is erroneous (at some point or other more or
less obvious) which any ordinary reader can, without
design, read improperly. It is the business of the poet
so to construct his line that the intention must be
caught at once. Even when these men have precisely
the same understanding of a sentence, they differ, and
often widely, in their modes of enunciating it. Any one
who has taken the trouble to examine the topic of em-
phasis (by which I here mean not accent of particular
syllables, but the dwelling on entire words), must have
seen that men emphasize in the most singularly arbi-

trary manner. There are certain large classes of people, for example, who persist in emphasizing their mono- syllables. Little uniformity of emphasis prevails; be- cause the thing itself—the idea, emphasis—is referable to no natural, at least to no well-comprehended and therefore uniform, law. Beyond a very narrow and vague limit the whole matter is conventionality. And if we differ in emphasis even when we agree in com- prehension, how much more so in the former when in the latter too! Apart, however, from the consideration of natural disagreement, is it not clear that, by trip- ping here and mouthing there, any sequence of words may be twisted into any species of rhythm? But are we thence to deduce that all sequences of words are rhythmical in a rational understanding of the term ?— for this is the deduction, precisely, to which the *reductio ad absurdum* will in the end bring all the propositions of Coleridge. Out of a hundred readers of *Christabel,* fifty will be able to make nothing of its rhythm, while forty-nine of the remaining fifty will, with some ado, fancy they comprehend it after the fourth or fifth peru- sal. The one out of the whole hundred who shall both comprehend and admire it at first sight must be an unaccountably clever person, and I am by far too modest to assume for a moment that that very clever person is myself.

In illustration of what is here advanced I cannot do better than quote a poem:

The Rationale of Verse

Pease porridge hot—pease porridge cold—
Pease porridge in the pot—nine days old.

Now those of my readers who have never heard this poem pronounced according to the nursery conventionality will find its rhythm as obscure as an explanatory note; while those who have heard it will divide it thus, declare it musical, and wonder how there can be any doubt about it.

Pease | porridge | hot | pease | porridge | cold |
Pease | porridge | in the | pot | nine | days | old. |

The chief thing in the way of this species of rhythm is the necessity which it imposes upon the poet of travelling in constant company with his compositions, so as to be ready at a moment's notice to avail himself of a well-understood poetical license—that of reading aloud one's own doggerel.

In Mr. Cranch's line,

Many are the | thoughts that | come to | me,

the general error of which I speak is, of course, very partially exemplified, and the purpose for which, chiefly, I cite it lies yet farther on in our topic.

The two divisions, "thoughts that" and "come to," are ordinary trochees. Of the last division, "me," we will talk hereafter. The first division, "many are the," would be thus accented by the Greek prosodies: "mānỹ ăre thĕ," and would be called by them ἀστρολόγος.

The Rationale of Verse

The Latin books would style the foot *poeon primus,* and both Greek and Latin would swear that it was composed of a trochee and what they term a pyrrhic; that is to say, a foot of two short syllables, a thing that cannot be, as I shall presently show.

But now there is an obvious difficulty. The *astrologos,* according to the prosodies' own showing, is equal to five short syllables and the trochee to three; yet, in the line quoted, these two feet are equal. They occupy precisely the same time. In fact, the whole music of the line depends upon their being made to occupy the same time. The prosodies, then, have demonstrated what all mathematicians have stupidly failed in demonstrating—that three and five are one and the same thing.

After what I have already said, however, about the bastard trochee and the bastard iambus, no one can have any trouble in understanding that " many are the " is of similar character. It is merely a bolder variation than usual from the routine of trochees, and introduces to the bastard trochee one additional syllable. But this syllable is not short. That is, it is not short in the sense of " short " as applied to the final syllable of the ordinary trochee, where the word means merely the half of long.

In this case (that of the additional syllable), " short," if used at all, must be used in the sense of the sixth of long. And all the three final syllables can be called

short only with the same understanding of the term.
The three together are equal only to the one short syl-
lable (whose place they supply) of the ordinary trochee.
It follows that there is no sense in thus (ᵕ) accenting
these syllables. We must devise for them some new
character which shall denote the sixth of long. Let it
be (ᴄ), the crescent placed with the curve to the left.
The whole foot, " mānȳ ăre thĕ," might be called a
" quick trochee."

We come now to the final division, " me," of Mr.
Cranch's line. It is clear that this foot, short as it
appears, is fully equal in time to each of the preceding.
It is, in fact, the cæsura, the foot which, in the begin-
ning of this paper, I called the most important in all
verse. Its chief office is that of pause or termination;
and here, at the end of a line, its use is easy, because
there is no danger of misapprehending its value. We
pause on it, by a seeming necessity, just as long as it
has taken us to pronounce the preceding feet, whether
iambuses, trochees, dactyls, or anapæsts. It is thus a
variable foot, and, with some care, may be well intro-
duced into the body of a line, as in a little poem of
great beauty by Mrs. Welby:

I have | a lit | tle step | s̄o̅n̅ | of on | ly three | years old.

Here we dwell on the cæsura, " son," just as long as it
requires us to pronounce either of the preceding or
succeeding iambuses. Its value, therefore, in this

line, is that of three short syllables. In the following dactylic line its value is that of four short syllables:

Pale as a | lily was | Emily | Gray.

I have accentuated the cæsura with a dotted line ($\cdots$) by way of expressing this variability of value.

I observed just now that there could be no such foot as one of two short syllables. What we start from in the very beginning of all idea on the topic of verse is quantity, length. Thus, when we enunciate an independent syllable it is long, as a matter of course. If we enunciate two, dwelling on both equally, we express equality in the enumeration or length, and have a right to call them two long syllables. If we dwell on one more than the other, we have also a right to call one short, because it is short in relation to the other. But if we dwell on both equally and with a tripping voice, saying to ourselves, here are two short syllables, the query might well be asked of us, " In relation to what are they short ?" Shortness is but the negation of length. To say, then, that two syllables, placed independently of any other syllable, are short, is merely to say that they have no positive length or enunciation, in other words that they are no syllables, that they do not exist at all. And if, persisting, we add anything about their equality, we are merely floundering in the idea of an identical equation, where, x being equal to x, nothing is shown to be equal to zero. In a word,

The Rationale of Verse

we can form no conception of a pyrrhic as of an independent foot. It is a mere chimera bred in the mad fancy of a pedant.

From what I have said about the equalization of the several feet of a line, it must not be deduced that any necessity for equality in time exists between the rhythm of several lines. A poem, or even a stanza, may begin with iambuses in the first line and proceed with anapæsts in the second, or even with the less accordant dactyls, as in the opening of quite a pretty specimen of verse by Miss Mary A. S. Aldrich:

> The wa | ter li | ly sleeps | in pride |
> Dōwn ĭn thĕ | dĕpths ŏf thĕ | āzūre | lāke.

Here " azure " is a spondee, equivalent to a dactyl; " lake," a cæsura.

I shall now best proceed in quoting the initial lines of Byron's *Bride of Abydos*:

> Know ye the land where the cypress and myrtle
>   Are emblems of deeds that are done in their clime,
> Where the rage of the vulture, the love of the turtle,
>   Now melt into softness, now madden to crime?
> Know ye the land of the cedar and vine,
> Where the flowers ever blossom, the beams ever shine,
> And the light wings of Zephyr, oppressed with perfume,
> Wax faint o'er the gardens of Gul in her bloom ?
> Where the citron and olive are fairest of fruit
> And the voice of the nightingale never is mute—
> Where the virgins are soft as the roses they twine,
> And all save the spirit of man is divine?

The Rationale of Verse

'T is the clime of the East; 't is the land of the Sun—
Can he smile on such deeds as his children have done?
Oh, wild as the accents of lovers' farewell
Are the hearts that they bear and the tales that they tell!

Now the flow of these lines, as times go, is very sweet and musical. They have been often admired, and justly,—as times go; that is to say, it is a rare thing to find better versification of its kind. And where verse is pleasant to the ear, it is silly to find fault with it because it refuses to be scanned. Yet I have heard men, professing to be scholars, who made no scruple of abusing these lines of Byron's on the ground that they were musical in spite of all law. Other gentlemen, not scholars, abused " all law " for the same reason; and it occurred neither to the one party nor to the other that the law about which they were disputing might possibly be no law at all—an ass of a law in the skin of a lion.

The grammars said something about dactylic lines, and it was easily seen that these lines were at least meant for dactylic. The first one was, therefore, thus divided:

Knŏw yĕ thĕ | lănd whĕre thĕ | cprĕss ănd | myrtlĕ. |

The concluding foot was a mystery; but the prosodies said something about the dactylic " measure " calling now and then for a double rhyme; and the court of inquiry were content to rest in the double rhyme, without exactly perceiving what a double rhyme had to do

257

with the question of an irregular foot. Quitting the first line, the second was thus scanned:

Arē ĕmblĕms | ŏf dĕeds thăt | āre dŏne ĭn | thĕir clĭme. |

It was immediately seen, however, that this would not do, it was at war with the whole emphasis of the reading. It could not be supposed that Byron, or any one in his senses, intended to place stress upon such monosyllables as " are," " of," and " their," nor could " their clime," collated with " to crime " in the corresponding line below, be fairly twisted into anything like a " double rhyme," so as to bring everything within the category of the grammars. But further these grammars spoke not. The inquirers, therefore, in spite of their sense of harmony in the lines, when considered without reference to scansion, fell back upon the idea that the " Are " was a blunder,—an excess for which the poet should be sent to Coventry,— and, striking it out, they scanned the remainder of the line as follows:

—— ēmblĕms ŏf | dĕeds thăt ăre | dŏne ĭn thĕir | clĭme. |

This answered pretty well; but the grammars admitted no such foot as a foot of one syllable; and, besides, the rhythm was dactylic. In despair, the books are well searched, however, and at last the investigators are gratified by a full solution of the riddle in the profound " observation " quoted in the beginning of this article: " When a syllable is wanting the verse is said to be

catalectic; when the measure is exact, the line is acata-
lectic; when there is a redundant syllable it forms
hypermeter." This is enough. The anomalous line
is pronounced to be catalectic at the head and to form
hypermeter at the tail, and so on, and so on; it being
soon discovered that nearly all the remaining lines are
in a similar predicament, and that what flows so
smoothly to the ear, although so roughly to the eye, is,
after all, a mere jumble of catalecticism, acatalecti-
cism, and hypermeter—not to say worse.

Now, had this court of inquiry been in possession of
even the shadow of the philosophy of verse, they would
have had no trouble in reconciling this oil and water
of the eye and ear by merely scanning the passage
without reference to lines, and continuously, thus:

Know ye the | land where the | cypress and | myrtle Are |
emblems of | deeds that are | done in their | clime Where
the | rage of the | vulture the | love of the | turtle Now |
melt into | softness now | madden to | *crime* | Know ye the |
land of the | cedar and | vine Where the | flowers ever |
blossom the | beams ever | shine Where the | light wings of |
Zephyr op | pressed with per | *fume Wax* | faint o'er the |
gardens of | Gul in her | bloom Where the | citron and |
olive are | fairest of | fruit And the | voice of the | nightin-
gale | never is | mute Where the | virgins are | soft as the |
roses they | *twine And* | all save the | spirit of | man is di |
vine 'T is the | clime of the | East 't is the | land of the | Sun
Can he | smile on such | deeds as his | children have | *done*
Oh | wild as the | accents of | lovers' fare | well Are the |
hearts that they | bear and the | tales that they | *tell,*

Here " crime " and " tell " (italicized) are cæsuras, each having the value of a dactyl, four short syllables; while " fume Wax," " twine And," and " done Oh " are spondees, which, of course, being composed of two long syllables, are also equal to four short, and are the dactyl's natural equivalent. The nicety of Byron's ear has led him into a succession of feet which, with two trivial exceptions as regards melody, are absolutely accurate—a very rare occurrence this in dactylic or anapæstic rhythms. The exceptions are found in the spondee " twine And," and the dactyl " smile on such." Both feet are false in point of melody. In " twine And," to make out the rhythm we must force " And " into a length which it will not naturally bear. We are called on to sacrifice either the proper length of the syllable as demanded by its position as a member of a spondee, or the customary accentuation of the word in conversation. There is no hesitation, and should be none. We at once give up the sound for the sense; and the rhythm is imperfect. In this instance it is very slightly so; not one person in ten thousand could, by ear, detect the inaccuracy. But the perfection of verse, as regards melody, consists in its never demanding any such sacrifice as is here demanded. The rhythmical must agree thoroughly with the reading flow. This perfection has in no instance been attained, but is unquestionably attainable. " Smile on such," the dactyl, is incorrect, because " such," from

The Rationale of Verse

the character of the two consonants " ch," cannot easily be enunciated in the ordinary time of a short syllable, which its position declares that it is. Almost every reader will be able to appreciate the slight difficulty here; and yet the error is by no means so important as that of the " And " in the spondee. By dexterity we may pronounce " such " in the true time; but the attempt to remedy the rhythmical deficiency of the " And " by drawing it out, merely aggravates the offence against natural enunciation by directing attention to the offence.

My main object, however, in quoting these lines, is to show that, in spite of the prosodies, the length of a line is entirely an arbitrary matter. We might divide the commencement of Byron's poem thus:

> Know ye the | land where the |

or thus:

> Know ye the | land where the | cypress and |

or thus:

> Know ye the | land where the | cypress and | myrtle are |

or thus:

> Know ye the | land where the | cypress and | myrtle are |
> emblems of |

In short, we may give it any division we please, and the lines will be good, provided we have at least two feet in a line. As in mathematics two units are required to form number, so rhythm (from the Greek

The Rationale of Verse

ἀριθμός, number) demands for its formation at least two feet.   Beyond doubt, we often see such lines as,

> Know ye the—
> Land where the—

lines of one foot; and our prosodies admit such, but with impropriety; for common sense would dictate that every so obvious division of a poem as is made by a line should include within itself all that is necessary for its own comprehension; but in a line of one foot we can have no appreciation of rhythm, which depends upon the equality between two or more pulsations.   The false lines, consisting sometimes of a single cæsura, which are seen in mock Pindaric odes, are of course rhythmical only in connection with some other line; and it is this want of independent rhythm which adapts them to the purposes of burlesque alone.   Their effect is that of incongruity (the principle of mirth), for they include the blankness of prose amid the harmony of verse.

My second object in quoting Byron's lines was that of showing how absurd it often is to cite a single line from amid the body of a poem, for the purpose of instancing the perfection or imperfection of the line's rhythm.   Were we to see by itself

> Know ye the land where the cypress and myrtle,

we might justly condemn it as defective in the final foot, which is equal to only three, instead of being equal to four, short syllables.

The Rationale of Verse

In the foot " flowers ever," we shall find a further exemplification of the principle of the bastard iambus, bastard trochee, and quick trochee, as I have been at some pains in describing these feet above. All the prosodies on English verse would insist upon making an elision in " flowers," thus, " flow'rs," but this is nonsense. In the quick trochee " mānȳ ărĕ thĕ," occurring in Mr. Cranch's trochaic line, we had to equalize the time of the three syllables, " many, are, the," to that of the one short syllable whose position they usurp. Accordingly each of these syllables is equal to the third of a short syllable; that is to say, the sixth of a long. But in Byron's dactylic rhythm we have to equalize the time of the three syllables, " ers, ev, er," to that of the one long syllable whose position they usurp, or (which is the same thing) of the two short. Therefore the value of each of the syllables " ers, ev, and er " is the third of a long. We enunciate them with only half the rapidity we employ in enunciating the three final syllables of the quick trochee, which latter is a rare foot. The " flowers ever," on the contrary, is as common in the dactylic rhythm as is the bastard trochee in the trochaic, or the bastard iambus in the iambic. We may as well accent it with the curve of the crescent to the right and call it a bastard dactyl. A bastard anapæst, whose nature I now need be at no trouble in explaining, will of course occur, now and then, in an anapæstic rhythm.

The Rationale of Verse

In order to avoid any chance of that confusion which is apt to be introduced in an essay of this kind by too sudden and radical an alteration of the conventionalities to which the reader has been accustomed, I have thought it right to suggest for the accent marks of the bastard trochee, bastard iambus, etc., certain characters which, in merely varying the direction of the ordinary short accent (˘), should imply (what is the fact) that the feet themselves are not new feet, in any proper sense, but simply modifications of the feet, respectively, from which they derive their names. Thus a bastard iambus is, in its essentiality, that is to say, in its time, an iambus. The variation lies only in the distribution of this time. The time, for example, occupied by the one short (or half of long) syllable, in the ordinary iambus, is, in the bastard, spread equally over two syllables, which are accordingly the fourth of long.

But this fact—the fact of the essentiality, or whole time, of the foot being unchanged—is now so fully before the reader that I may venture to propose, finally, an accentuation which shall answer the real purpose, that is to say, what should be the real purpose of all accentuation,—the purpose of expressing to the eye the exact relative value of every syllable employed in verse.

I have already shown that enunciation, or length, is the point from which we start. In other words, we begin with a long syllable. This, then, is our unit; and

there will be no need of accenting it at all. An un-
accented syllable in a system of accentuation is to be
regarded always as a long syllable. Thus a spondee
would be without accent. In an iambus, the first
syllable, being short, or the half of long, should be
accented with a small 2, placed beneath the syllable;
the last syllable, being long, should be unaccented;
the whole would be thus: control. In a trochee these
                              2
accents would be merely conversed; thus, manly. In
                                             2
a dactyl each of the two final syllables, being the half
of long, should also be accented with a small 2 beneath
the syllable; and, the first syllable left unaccented, the
whole would be thus: happiness. In an anapæst we
                          2 2
should converse the dactyl; thus, in the land. In the
                                       2   2
bastard dactyl, each of the three concluding syllables,
being the third of long, should be accented with a
small 3 beneath the syllable, and the whole foot would
stand thus: flowers ever. In the bastard anapæst we
            3   3 3
should converse the bastard dactyl; thus, in the re-
                                         3   3   3
bound. In the bastard iambus, each of the two initial
syllables, being the fourth of long, should be accented
below with a small 4; the whole foot would be thus:
in the rain. In the bastard trochee we should con-
   4   4
verse the bastard iambus; thus, many a. In the quick
                                      4 4
trochee, each of the three concluding syllables, being
the sixth of long, should be accented below with a

small 6; the whole foot would be thus: $\underset{6}{\text{ma}}\underset{6}{\text{ny}} \underset{6}{\text{are the}}$.
The quick iambus is not yet created, and most prob-
ably never will be, for it will be excessively useless,
awkward, and liable to misconception,—as I have
already shown that even the quick trochee is,—but,
should it appear, we must accent it by conversing the
quick trochee. The cæsura, being variable in length,
but always longer than " long," should be accented
above, with a number expressing the length or value
of the distinctive foot of the rhythm in which it occurs.
Thus a cæsura occurring in a spondaic rhythm would
be accented with a small 2 above the syllable, or,
rather, foot. Occurring in a dactylic or anapæstic
rhythm, we also accent it with the 2 above the foot.
Occurring in an iambic rhythm, however, it must be
accented above with $1\frac{1}{2}$, for this is the relative value
of the iambus. Occurring in the trochaic rhythm, we
give it, of course, the same accentuation. For the
complex $1\frac{1}{2}$, however, it would be advisable to sub-
stitute the simpler expression, $\frac{3}{2}$, which amounts to
the same thing.

In this system of accentuation Mr. Cranch's lines,
quoted above, would thus be written:

Many are the | thoughts that | come to | $\overset{\frac{3}{2}}{\text{me}}$
$\quad\;\underset{6}{\;}\;\;\underset{6}{\;}\;\;\underset{6}{\;}\qquad\qquad\underset{2}{\;}\qquad\qquad\underset{2}{\;}$
In my | lonely | musing, |
$\;\;\underset{2}{\;}\qquad\underset{2}{\;}\qquad\underset{2}{\;}$

And they | drift so | strange and | $\overset{\frac{3}{2}}{\text{swift}}$
$\;\;\underset{2}{\;}\qquad\;\underset{2}{\;}\qquad\quad\underset{2}{\;}$
There 's no | time for | choosing
$\quad\underset{2}{\;}\qquad\;\underset{2}{\;}\qquad\underset{2}{\;}$

The Rationale of Verse

Which to | follow, | for to | leave
   2   2   2
Any | seems a | losing.
 2   2   2

In the ordinary system the accentuation would be thus:

Mănÿ arĕ thĕ | thōughts thăt | cōme tŏ | mĕ
  Ĭn mÿ | lōnelÿ | mūsĭng,
Ānd thĕy | drīft sŏ | strānge ănd | swĭft
  Thĕre 's nŏ | tīme fŏr | choōsĭng
Whĭch tŏ | fōllŏw, | fōr tŏ | lĕave
  Ānÿ | sēems ă | lōsĭng.

It must be observed here that I do not grant this to be the " ordinary " scansion. On the contrary, I never yet met the man who had the faintest comprehension of the true scanning of these lines, or of such as these. But granting this to be the mode in which our prosodies would divide the feet, they would accentuate the syllables as just above.

Now, let any reasonable person compare the two modes. The first advantage seen in my mode is that of simplicity—of time, labor, and ink saved. Counting the fractions as two accents, even, there will be found only twenty-six accents to the stanza. In the common accentuation there are forty-one. But admit that all this is a trifle, which it is not, and let us proceed to points of importance. Does the common accentuation express the truth in particular, in general, or in any regard ? Is it consistent with itself ? Does

The Rationale of Verse

it convey either to the ignorant or to the scholar a just conception of the rhythm of the lines ? Each of these questions must be answered in the negative. The crescents, being precisely similar, must be understood as expressing, all of them, one and the same thing; and so all prosodies have always understood them and wished them to be understood. They express, indeed, " short "; but this word has all kinds of meanings. It serves to represent (the reader is left to guess when) sometimes the half, sometimes the third, sometimes the fourth, sometimes the sixth of " long "; while " long " itself in the books is left undefined and undescribed. On the other hand, the horizontal accent, it may be said, expresses sufficiently well and unvaryingly the syllables which are meant to be long. It does nothing of the kind. This horizontal accent is placed over the cæsura (wherever, as in the Latin prosodies, the cæsura is recognized) as well as over the ordinary long syllable, and implies anything and everything, just as the crescent. But grant that it does express the ordinary long syllables (leaving the cæsura out of the question), have I not given the identical expression by not employing any expression at all ? In a word, while the prosodies, with a certain number of accents express precisely nothing whatever, I, with scarcely half the number, have expressed everything which, in a system of accentuation, demands expression. In glancing at my mode in the lines of Mr.

The Rationale of Verse

Cranch it will be seen that it conveys not only the exact relation of the syllables and feet among themselves in those particular lines, but their precise value in relation to any other existing or conceivable feet or syllables in any existing or conceivable system of rhythm.

The object of what we call scansion is the distinct marking of the rhythmical flow. Scansion with accents or perpendicular lines between the feet—that is to say, scansion by the voice only—is scansion to the ear only; and all very good in its way. The written scansion addresses the ear through the eye. In either case the object is the distinct marking of the rhythmical, musical, or reading flow. There can be no other object, and there is none. Of course, then, the scansion and the reading flow should go hand-in-hand. The former must agree with the latter. The former represents and expresses the latter; and is good or bad as it truly or falsely represents and expresses it. If by the written scansion of a line we are not enabled to perceive any rhythm or music in the line, then either the line is unrhythmical or the scansion false. Apply all this to the English lines which we have quoted at various points in the course of this article. It will be found that the scansion exactly conveys the rhythm, and thus thoroughly fulfils the only purpose for which scansion is required.

But let the scansion of the schools be applied to the Greek and Latin verse, and what result do we find ?—

that the verse is one thing and the scansion quite another. The ancient verse, read aloud, is in general musical, and occasionally very musical. Scanned by the prosodial rules we can, for the most part, make nothing of it whatever. In the case of the English verse, the more emphatically we dwell on the divisions between the feet, the more distinct is our perception of the kind of rhythm intended. In the case of the Greek and Latin, the more we dwell the less distinct is this perception. To make this clear by an example:

> Mæcenas, atavis edite regibus,
> O, et præsidium et dulce decus meum,
> Sunt quos curriculo pulverem Olympicum
> Collegisse juvat, metaque fervidis
> Evitata rotis, palmaque nobilis
> Terrarum dominos evehit ad Deos.

Now, in reading these lines there is scarcely one person in a thousand who, if even ignorant of Latin, will not immediately feel and appreciate their flow, their music. A prosodist, however, informs the public that the scansion runs thus:

> Mæce | nas ata | vis | edite | regibus
> O et | præsidi' | et | dulce de | cus meum
> Sunt quos | curricu | lo | pulver' O | lympicum
> Colle | gisse ju | vat | metaque | fervidis
> Evi | tata ro | tis | palmaque | nobilis
> Terra | rum domi | nos | evehit | ad Deos.

The Rationale of Verse

Now, I do not deny that we get a certain sort of music from the lines if we read them according to this scansion; but I wish to call attention to the fact that this scansion, and the certain sort of music which grows out of it, are entirely at war not only with the reading flow which any ordinary person would naturally give the lines, but with the reading flow universally given them, and never denied them, by even the most obstinate and stolid of scholars.

And now these questions are forced upon us: " Why exists this discrepancy between the modern verse with its scansion and the ancient verse with its scansion ? " —" Why, in the former case, are there agreement and representation, while in the latter there is neither the one nor the other ? " or, to come to the point, " How are we to reconcile the ancient verse with the scholastic scansion of it ? " This absolutely necessary conciliation—shall we bring it about by supposing the scholastic scansion wrong because the ancient verse is right, or by maintaining that the ancient verse is wrong because the scholastic scansion is not to be gainsaid ?

Were we to adopt the latter mode of arranging the difficulty, we might, in some measure, at least simplify the expression of the arrangement by putting it thus: Because the pedants have no eyes, therefore the old poets had no ears.

" But," say the gentlemen without the eyes, " the scholastic scansion, although certainly not handed down to us in form from the old poets themselves (the gentlemen without the ears), is nevertheless deduced from certain facts which are supplied us by careful observation of the old poems."

And let us illustrate this strong position by an example from an American poet, who must be a poet of some eminence or he will not answer the purpose. Let us take Mr. Alfred B. Street. I remember these two lines of his:

> His sinuous path, by blazes, wound
> Among trunks grouped in myriads round.

With the sense of these lines I have nothing to do. When a poet is in a " fine frenzy," he may as well imagine a large forest as a small one; and " by blazes " is not intended for an oath. My concern is with the rhythm, which is iambic.

Now let us suppose that a thousand years hence, when the " American language " is dead, a learned prosodist should be deducing, from " careful observation " of our best poets, a system of scansion for our poetry. And let us suppose that this prosodist had so little dependence in the generality and immutability of the laws of Nature as to assume in the outset, that, because we lived a thousand years before his time, and made use of steam-engines instead of mesmeric balloons, we must therefore have had a very singular fashion of mouthing our vowels and altogether

The Rationale of Verse

of Hudsonizing our verse. And let us suppose that with these and other fundamental propositions carefully put away in his brain, he should arrive at the line,

Among | trunks grouped | in my | riads round.

Finding it an obviously iambic rhythm, he would divide it as above; and observing that " trunks " made the first member of an iambus, he would call it short, as Mr. Street intended it to be. Now further, if, instead of admitting the possibility that Mr. Street (who by that time would be called Street simply, just as we say Homer)—that Mr. Street might have been in the habit of writing carelessly, as the poets of the prosodist's own era did, and as all poets will do (on account of being geniuses),—instead of admitting this, suppose the learned scholar should make a " rule " and put it in a book, to the effect that in the American verse the vowel " u," when found imbedded among nine consonants, was short; what, under such circumstances, would the sensible people of the scholar's day have a right not only to think, but to say, of that scholar ?—why, that he was " a fool—by blazes! "

I have put an extreme case, but it strikes at the root of the error. The " rules " are grounded in " authority "; and this " authority "—can any one tell us what it means ? or can any one suggest anything that it may not mean ? Is it not clear that the " scholar " above referred to might as readily have deduced from

The Rationale of Verse

authority a totally false system as a partially true one ?
To deduce from authority a consistent prosody of the
ancient metres would indeed have been within the
limits of the barest possibility; and the task has *not*
been accomplished for the reason that it demands a
species of ratiocination altogether out of keeping with
the brain of a bookworm. A rigid scrutiny will show
that the very few " rules " which have not as many
exceptions as examples, are those which have, by
accident, their true bases not in authority, but in the
omniprevalent laws of syllabification; such, for exam-
ple, as the rule which declares a vowel before two con-
sonants to be long.

In a word, the gross confusion and antagonism of
the scholastic prosody, as well as its marked inappli-
cability to the reading flow of the rhythms it pretends
to illustrate, are attributable, first, to the utter absence
of natural principle as a guide in the investigations
which have been undertaken by inadequate men; and,
secondly, to the neglect of the obvious consideration
that the ancient poems, which have been the criteria
throughout, were the work of men who must have
written as loosely, and with as little definitive system
as ourselves.

Were Horace alive to-day he would divide for us
his first Ode thus, and make " great eyes " when
assured by prosodists that he had no business to make
any such division!

The Rationale of Verse

Mæcenas | atavis | edite | regibus
  2 2   2 2   2 2   2 2

O et præ | sidium et | dulce de | cus meum
 2 2   3 3 3   2 2   2 2

Sunt quos cur | riculo | pulverem O | lympicum
 2   2   2 2   3 3 3   2   2

Collegisse | juvat | metaque | fervidis
 3 3 3   2 2   2 2

Evitata | rotis | palmaque | nobilis
 3 3 3   2 2   2 2

Terrarum | dominos | evehit | ad Deos.
 2 2   2 2   2 2   2 2

Read by this scansion the flow is preserved; and the more we dwell on the divisions the more the intended rhythm becomes apparent. Moreover, the feet have all the same time; while, in the scholastic scansion, trochees—admitted trochees—are absurdly employed as equivalents to spondees and dactyls. The books declare, for instance, that " Colle," which begins the fourth line, is a trochee, and seem to be gloriously unconscious that to put a trochee in opposition with a longer foot is to violate the inviolable principle of all music, time.

It will be said, however, by " some people," that I have no business to make a dactyl out of such obviously long syllables as " sunt, quos, cur." Certainly I have no business to do so. I never do so. And Horace should not have done so. But he did. Mr. Bryant and Mr. Longfellow do the same thing every day. And merely because these gentlemen, now and then, forget themselves in this way, it would be hard if some future prosodist should insist upon twisting the *Thanatopsis*

or the *Spanish Student* into a jumble of trochees, spon-
dees, and dactyls.

It may be said, also, by some other people, that in
the word " decus " I have succeeded no better than the
books in making the scansional agree with the reading
flow; and that " decus " was not pronounced " de*cus*."
I reply, that there can be no doubt of the word having
been pronounced, in this case, " de*cus*." It must be
observed that the Latin inflection, or variation of a
word in its terminating syllable, caused the Romans—
must have caused them—to pay greater attention to
the termination of a word than to its commencement,
or than we do to the terminations of our words. The
end of the Latin word established that relation of the
word with other words which we establish by preposi-
tions or auxiliary verbs. Therefore, it would seem
infinitely less odd to them than it does to us to dwell
at any time, for any slight purpose, abnormally, on a
terminating syllable. In verse, this license—scarcely
a license—would be frequently admitted. These ideas
unlock the secret of such lines as the

> Litoreis ingens inventa sub ilici*bus sus,*

and the

> Parturiunt montes et nascitur ridicu*lus mus,*

which I quoted, some time ago, while speaking of rhyme.

As regards the prosodial elisions, such as that of "rem"
before " O," in " pulverem Olympicum," it is really
difficult to understand how so dismally silly a notion

The Rationale of Verse

could have entered the brain even of a pedant. Were it demanded of me why the books cut off one vowel before another, I might say: It is, perhaps, because the books think that, since a bad reader is so apt to slide the one vowel into the other at any rate, it is just as well to print them ready-slided. But in the case of the terminating " m," which is the most readily pronounced of all consonants (as the infantile " mamma " will testify), and the most impossible to cheat the ear of by any system of sliding—in the case of the " m," I should be driven to reply that, to the best of my belief, the prosodists did the thing because they had a fancy for doing it, and wished to see how funny it would look after it was done. The thinking reader will perceive that, from the great facility with which " em " may be enunciated, it is admirably suited to form one of the rapid short syllables in the bastard dactyl (" pulverem O "); but because the books had no conception of a bastard dactyl, they knocked it on the head at once— by cutting off its tail!

Let me now give a specimen of the true scansion of another Horatian measure—embodying an instance of proper elision.

Integer | vitæ | scelerisque | purus |
  2 2   3   3   3
Non eget | Mauri | jaculis ne | que arcu
  2 2   3   3   3
Nec vene | natis | gravida sa | gittis |
  2 2   3   3   3
      Fusce pha | retrâ.
        2   2

The Rationale of Verse

Here the regular recurrence of the bastard dactyl gives great animation to the rhythm. The " e " before the " a " in " que arcu," is, almost of sheer necessity, cut off; that is to say, run into the " a " so as to preserve the spondee. But even this license it would have been better not to take.

Had I space, nothing would afford me greater pleasure than to proceed with the scansion of all the ancient rhythms, and to show how easily, by the help of common sense, the intended music of each and all can be rendered instantaneously apparent. But I have already overstepped my limits, and must bring this paper to an end.

It will never do, however, to omit all mention of the heroic hexameter.

I began the " processes " by a suggestion of the spondee as the first step toward verse. But the innate monotony of the spondee has caused its disappearance, as the basis of rhythm, from all modern poetry. We may say, indeed, that the French heroic, the most wretchedly monotonous verse in existence, is, to all intents and purposes, spondaic. But it is not designedly spondaic, and if the French were ever to examine it at all, they would no doubt pronounce it iambic. It must be observed that the French language is strangely peculiar in this point—that it is without accentuation, and consequently without verse. The genius of the people, rather than the structure of the tongue, declares that their words are, for the most part, enunciated with a uniform dwelling on each syllable. For example, we say " syl*labification*." A Frenchman would say " syl-la-bi-fi-ca-ti-on," dwelling on no one of the syllables with any noticeable particularity. Here again I put an extreme case, in order to be well understood; but the general fact is as I give it—that, comparatively, the French have no accentuation. And there can be nothing worth the name of verse without. Therefore, the French have no verse worth the name— which is the fact, put in sufficiently plain terms. Their iambic rhythm so superabounds in absolute spondees as to warrant me in calling its basis spondaic; but French is the only modern tongue which has any rhythm with such basis; and even in the French, it is, as I have said, unintentional.

Admitting, however, the validity of my suggestion, that the spondee was the first approach to verse, we should expect to find, first, natural spondees (words each forming just a spondee) most abundant in the most ancient languages; and, secondly, we should expect to find spondees forming the basis of the most ancient rhythms. These expectations are in both cases confirmed.

Of the Greek hexameter, the intentional basis is spondaic. The dactyls are the variation of the theme. It will be observed that there is no absolute certainty about their points of interposition. The penultimate

foot, it is true, is usually a dactyl, but not uniformly
so; while the ultimate, on which the ear lingers, is
always a spondee. Even that the penultimate is usu-
ally a dactyl may be clearly referred to the necessity
of winding up with the distinctive spondee. In cor-
roboration of this idea, again, we should look to find
the penultimate spondee most usual in the most
ancient verse; and, accordingly, we find it more fre-
quent in the Greek than in the Latin hexameter.

But besides all this, spondees are not only more
prevalent in the heroic hexameter than dactyls, but
occur to such an extent as is even unpleasant to mod-
ern ears, on account of monotony. What the modern
chiefly appreciates and admires in the Greek hexam-
ter is the melody of the abundant vowel sounds.
The Latin hexameters really please very few moderns,
although so many pretend to fall into ecstasies about
them. In the hexameters quoted, several pages ago,
from Silius Italicus, the preponderance of the spondee
is strikingly manifest. Besides the natural spondees
of the Greek and Latin, numerous artificial ones arise
in the verse of these tongues on account of the ten-
dency which inflection has, to throw full accentuation
on terminal syllables; and the preponderance of the
spondee is further insured by the comparative infre-
quency of the small prepositions which we have to
serve us instead of case, and also the absence of the
diminutive auxiliary verbs with which we have to eke

The Rationale of Verse

out the expression of our primary ones. These are the monosyllables whose abundance serve to stamp the poetic genius of a language as tripping, or dactylic.

Now, paying no attention to these facts, Sir Philip Sidney, Professor Longfellow, and innumerable other persons more or less modern, have busied themselves in constructing what they suppose to be " English hexameters on the model of the Greek." The only difficulty was that (even leaving out of question the melodious masses of vowels) these gentlemen never could get their English hexameters to sound Greek. Did they look Greek ?—that should have been the query; and the reply might have led to a solution of the riddle. In placing a copy of ancient hexameters side by side with a copy, in similar type, of such hexameters as Professor Longfellow, or Professor Felton, or the Frogpondian professors collectively, are in the shameful practice of composing " on the model of the Greek," it will be seen that the latter (hexameters, not professors) are about one third longer to the eye, on an average, than the former. The more abundant dactyls make the difference. And it is the greater number of spondees in the Greek than in the English, in the ancient than in the modern tongue, which has caused it to fall out that while these eminent scholars were groping about in the dark for a Greek hexameter, which is a spondaic rhythm varied now and then by dactyls, they merely stumbled, to the lasting scandal of scholarship, over something which, on account of its long-leggedness, we may as well term a Feltonian hexameter, and which is a dactylic rhythm, interrupted, rarely, by artificial spondees which are no spondees at all, and which are curiously thrown in by the heels at all kinds of improper and impertinent points.

Here is a specimen of the Longfellownian hexameter:

Also the | church with | in was a | dorned for | this was the | season
In which the | young their | parents' | hope and the | loved ones of | Heaven
Should at the | foot of the | altar re | new the | vows of their | baptism
Therefore each | nook and | corner was | swept and | cleaned and the | dust was
Blown from the | walls and | ceiling and | from the | oil-painted | benches.

Mr. Longfellow is a man of imagination; but can he imagine that any individual, with a proper understanding of the danger of lockjaw, would make the attempt of twisting his mouth into the shape necessary for the emission of such spondees as " par*ents*," and " from the," or such dactyls as " cleaned and the," and " loved ones of " ?   " Baptism " is by no means a bad spondee, perhaps because it happens to be a dactyl; of all the rest, however, I am dreadfully ashamed.

The Rationale of Verse

But these feet, dactyls and spondees, all together, should thus be put at once into their proper position:

Also, the church within was adorned; for this was the season in which the young, their parents' hope, and the loved ones of Heaven, should, at the foot of the altar, renew the vows of their baptism. Therefore each nook and corner was swept and cleaned; and the dust was blown from the walls and ceiling, and from the oil-painted benches.

There! That is respectable prose; and it will incur no danger of ever getting its character ruined by anybody's mistaking it for verse.

But even when we let these modern hexameters go, as Greek, and merely hold them fast in their proper character of Longfellownian, or Feltonian, or Frogpondian, we must still condemn them as having been committed in a radical misconception of the philosophy of verse. The spondee, as I observed, is the theme of the Greek line. Most of the ancient hexameters begin with spondees, for the reason that the spondee is the theme; and the ear is filled with it as with a burden. Now the Feltonian dactylics have, in the same way, dactyls for the theme, and most of them begin with dactyls,—which is all very proper if not very Greek; but, unhappily, the one point at which they are very Greek is that point, precisely, at which they should be nothing but Feltonian. They always close with what is meant for a spondee. To be consistently silly, they should die off in a dactyl.

The Rationale of Verse

That a truly Greek hexameter cannot, however, be readily composed in English, is a proposition which I am by no means inclined to admit. I think I could manage the point myself. For example:

Do tell! | when may we | hope to make | men of sense | out
    of the | Pundits
Born and brought | up with their | snouts deep | down in the |
    mud of the | Frog-pond ?
Why ask ? | who ever | yet saw | money made | out of a | fat
    old
Jew, or | downright | upright | nutmegs | out of a | pine-knot ?

The proper spondee predominance is here preserved. Some of the dactyls are not so good as I could wish, but, upon the whole, the rhythm is very decent, to say nothing of its excellent sense.

Notes on English Verse [1]

FEW questions of equal importance have received so little attention as the rationale of rhythm in general. The Greek and the Latin prosodies have their rules, but nothing more. The philosophy of these rules is untouched. No one

[1] To the third and last (March, 1843) number of that short-lived and now very rare Boston monthly, *The Pioneer,* edited by James Russell Lowell and Robert Carter, Poe contributed an article entitled " Notes Upon English Verse." This paper, which the author highly valued, also did duty as a lecture, and was recast for the discussion of " The Rationale of Verse," in the collected works. It seems desirable to reprint from *The Pioneer* the portions of the magazine paper which were subsequently omitted, as they are reasonably complete in themselves, and form a valuable addition to Poe's theories on versification. They are also interesting as presenting a scansion-scheme of Holmes's *The Last Leaf,* which will seem incorrect to most students of metrics. This part of the manuscript of the *Pioneer* article was subsequently given to Dr. Holmes by Mr. Carter, who had apparently forgotten how it came into his possession; and it was printed as previously unpublished matter in an illustrated edition (1885) of *The Last Leaf.* Dr. Holmes wrote on 6th November, 1885, in response to a query as to Poe's theory of the construction of the verses in question:. " I wish I had time . . . to go into the question . . . as to the scansion of the poem. I never studied the verses from that point of view, trusting wholly to my ear and leaving the analysis of my lines to those who thought them worth it."
In the following pages one quotation is repeated from " The Rationale of Verse," as necessary to the sense; but the remainder of the matter is different.

Notes on English Verse

has thought of reducing rule, in general, to its lowest terms, to its ultimate expression in law. I have long thought that it is only by an analysis such as is here suggested, with disregard, for the time, of the mere conventionalities and unwarranted assumptions which disgrace our treatises on the ancient rhythms, that we shall be able to arrive, if ever, at any intelligible view of these rhythms themselves. Quantity is a point in the investigation of which the lumber of mere learning may be dispensed with, if ever in any. Its appreciation is universal. It appertains to no region, nor race, nor era in especial. To melody and to harmony the Greeks hearkened with ears precisely similar to those which we employ, for similar purposes, at present; and a pendulum at Athens would have vibrated much after the same fashion as does a pendulum in the city of Penn.

But while a full and unpedantic discussion of metre in general is much needed, the purpose of this article extends no farther than to some practical observations on the English rhythms ; and I am led to these observations solely by the hope of supplying, to some extent, the singular deficiency of our ordinary treatises on the topic. . . .

The word " verse " is derived (through *versus*) from the Latin *verto,* I turn, and has reference to the turning at the end of the line and commencing anew with a capital letter. It can be nothing but this derivation

Notes on English Verse

which has led to the error of our writers upon prosody. It is this which has seduced them into regarding the line itself—the *versus,* or turning—as an essential, or principle, of metre; and hence the term " versification " has been employed as sufficiently general, or inclusive, for treatises upon rhythm in general. Hence, also, the precise catalogue of a few varieties of English lines, when these varieties are, in fact, almost without limit.

I shall dismiss entirely from the consideration of the principle of rhythm the idea of versification, or the construction of verse. In so doing we shall avoid a world of confusion. Verse is, indeed, an afterthought, or an embellishment, or an improvement, rather than an element of rhythm; and this is the fact which, perhaps, more than anything else, has induced the easy admission into the realms of poesy of such works as the *Télémaque* of Fénelon. In the elaborate modulation of their sentences they fulfil the idea of metre; and their arrangement, or rather their division, into lines, which could be readily effected, would do little more than present this idea in a popularly intelligible dress.

Holding these things in view, the prosodist who rightly examines that which constitutes the external, or most immediately recognizable, form of poetry will commence with the definition of rhythm. Now rhythm, from the Greek ἄριθμος, number, is a term which, in its present application, very nearly conveys its own idea. No more proper word could be employed to present the conception intended; for rhythm, in prosody, is, in its last analysis, identical with time in music. For this reason I have used, throughout this article, as synonymous with rhythm, the word " metre," from μέτρον, measure. Either the one or the other may be defined as " the arrangement of words into two or more consecutive, equal, pulsations of time." These pulsations are feet. Two feet, at least, are requisite to constitute a rhythm; just as, in mathematics, two units are necessary to form number. The syllables of which the foot consists, when the foot is not a syllable in itself, are subdivisions of the pulsations. No equality is demanded in these subdivisions. It is only required that, so far as regards two consecutive feet at least, the sum of the times of the syllables in one shall be equal to the sum of the times of the syllables in the other. Beyond two pulsations there is no necessity for equality of time. All beyond is arbitrary or conventional. A third and fourth pulsation may embody half, or double, or any proportion of the time occupied in the two first.

I have already said that all syllables, in metre, are either long or short. Our usual prosodies maintain that a long syllable is equal, in its time, to two short; this, however, is but an approach to the truth. It should be here observed that the quantity of an English syllable has no dependence upon the sound of its vowel or diphthong, but chiefly upon accentuation. Monosyllables are exceedingly variable, and, for the most part, may be either long or short, to suit the demand of the rhythm. In polysyllables, the accented ones are always long, while those which immediately precede or succeed them are always short. Emphasis will render any short syllable long.

Rhythm being thus understood, the prosodist should proceed to define versification as the making of verses, and verse as the " arbitrary or conventional isolation of rhythms into masses of greater or less extent."

Let us now exemplify what has been said. We will take the words,

Ĭ ăm mōnărch,

with the accentuation which belongs to them in the well-known line,

Ĭ ăm mōnărch ŏf āll Ĭ sŭrvēy.

Of the three first words, by themselves, with the accentuation as here given, we can form no metre or rhythm. We cannot divide them into " two or more equal pulsations of time," that is to say, into two metrical feet. If we divide them thus:

Ĭ ăm | mōnărch,

the time of the latter division is to that of the former as three to two; and a glance will suffice to show that

Notes on English Verse

no nearer approach to equal division is practicable. The words as they stand, therefore, are purely prose. But, by placing an emphasis upon the pronoun, we double its length, and the whole is resolved into rhythm; for

I am monarch

is readily divided into two equal pulsations, thus:

Ĭ ăm | mōnărch.

These equal pulsations are trochaic feet; and, from the appreciation of such equality as we recognize in them arises the gratification of rhythm. With less than two feet there can be no comparison, thus no equality, thus no rhythm. " But no equality is demanded " (here I quote my previous words) " in the subdivisions of the rhythm. It is only required that the sum of the times of the syllables in the one shall be equal to the sum of the times of the syllables in the other," as we see it above. The entire line,

I am monarch of all I survey,

is thus scanned:

Ĭ ăm mōn | ărch ŏf āll | Ĭ sŭrvēy.

Here are three anapæsts. The two first suffice to establish a rhythm; but the third confirms it. Had the words run thus:

I am monarch of all I see,

Notes on English Verse

no ear would have been materially offended; but it is evident that, in this case, we should have thus scanned the verse:

Ĭ ăm mōn-| ărch ŏf āll | Ī sĕe;

and the last foot, being a pure spondee (two long syllables, equal to the one long and two short syllables of the preceding anapæsts), is, of itself, sufficient demonstration that the spondee has been improperly rejected from the English rhythms.

The two anapæsts

Ĭ ăm mōn- | ărch ŏf āll,

do not demand that, if a third foot succeed, this third foot be an anapæst, or even the equivalent in time of an anapæst. The requisitions of rhythm are fulfilled in the two; and a novel mood of metre may now arise. A conventionality, however, founded in reason, has decided that the new metre should, in general, form the commencement of a new line, that the ear may thus, by means of the eye, be prepared for the change. The cæsura, whose peculiarities have never been discussed, and which I have already described as a foot consisting of a single long syllable, is frequently found interposed (especially in ancient metres) between various rhythms in the same line. Its object, in such situations, is to allow time, or opportunity, for the lapse from one rhythm to another, or, more ordinarily, from a rhythm to a variation of the same. . . .

One word here in regard to rhyme. Its employment is quite as arbitrary as that of verse itself. Our books speak of it as " a similarity of sound between the last syllables of different lines." But how absurd such definition, in the very teeth of the admitted facts that rhymes are often used in the middle of verses, and that mere similarity of sound is insufficient to constitute them in perfection. Rhyme may be defined as " identity of sound occurring among rhythms, between syllables or portions of syllables of equal length, at equal intervals, or at interspaces the multiples of these intervals."

The iambic, the trochaic, the anapæstic, and the dactylic are the usually admitted divisions of English verse. These varieties, in their purity, or perfection, are to be understood as mere indefinite successions of the feet or pulsations, respectively, from which are derived their names. Our prosodies cite examples of only the most common divisions of the respective rhythms into lines, but profess to cite instances of all the varieties of English verse. These varieties are, nevertheless, unlimited, as will be readily seen from what has been said; but the books have done much, by their dogmas, in the way of prohibiting invention. A wide field is open for its display in novel combinations of metre. The immenseness of the effect deriv-

Notes on English Verse

able from the harmonious combination of various rhythms is a point strangely neglected or misunderstood. We have, in America, some few versifiers of fine ear, who succeed to admiration in the building of the ordinary established lines,—the iambic pentameters of Sprague, for example, surpass even those of Pope; but we have had few evidences of originality in the division of the old rhythms or in the combination of their varieties. In general, the grossest ignorance prevails, even among our finest poets, and even in respect to the commonplace harmonies upon which they are most habitually employed. If we regard at the same time accuracy of rhythm, melody, and invention, or novel combination, of metre, I should have no hesitation in saying that a young and true poetess of Kentucky, Mrs. Amelia Welby, has done more in the way of really good verse than any individual among us. I shall be pardoned, nevertheless, for quoting and commenting upon an excellently well-conceived and well-managed specimen of versification, which will aid in developing some of the propositions already expressed. It is the *Last Leaf* of Oliver W. Holmes:

> I saw him once before,
> As he passed by the door,
>   And again
> The pavement stones resound
> As he totters o'er the ground
>   With his cane.

Notes on English Verse

They say that in his prime,
Ere the pruning-knife of Time
    Cut him down,
Not a better man was found
By the crier on his round
    Through the town.

But now he walks the streets,
And he looks at all he meets
    So forlorn;
And he shakes his feeble head
That it seems as if he said,
    They are gone.

The mossy marbles rest
On the lips that he has prest
    In their bloom;
And the names he loved to hear
Have been carved for many a year
    On the tomb.

My grandmamma has said,—
Poor old lady! she is dead
    Long ago,—
That he had a Roman nose,
And his cheek was like a rose
    In the snow.

But now his nose is thin,
And it rests upon his chin
    Like a staff;
And a crook is in his back,
And a melancholy crack
    In his laugh.

Notes on English Verse

I know it is a sin
For me to sit and grin
    At him here;
But the old three-corner'd hat,
And the breeches, and all that,
    Are so queer!

And if I should live to be
The last leaf upon the tree
    In the spring,
Let them smile, as I do now,
At the old forsaken bough
    Where I cling.

Every one will acknowledge the effective harmony of these lines; yet the attempt to scan them by any reference to the rules of our prosodies will be vain. Indeed, I am at a loss to imagine what these books could say upon the subject that would not immediately contradict all that has been said by them upon others. Let us scan the first stanza:

Ĭ sāw | hĭm ōnce | bĕfŏre
Ās hĕ | pāssĕd | bȳ thĕ | dōor
    Ānd ă- | gāin
Thĕ pāve | mĕnt stōnes | rĕsŏund
Ās hĕ | tōttĕrs | ŏ'er thĕ | grŏund
    Wĭth hĭs | cāne.

This is the general scansion of the poem. We have, first, three iambuses. The second line shifts the rhythm into the trochaic, giving us three trochees,

Notes on English Verse

wĭth a cæsura, equivalent, in this case, to a trochee.
The third line is a trochee and equivalent cæsura.
But it must be observed that, although the cæsura is
variable in value, and can thus be understood as
equivalent to any pulsation which precedes it, it is
insufficient to form, with any single pulsation, a per-
fect rhythm. The rhythm of the line " and again " is
referable, therefore, to the line preceding, and depen-
dent thereupon. The whole would have been more
properly written thus:

> I sāw | hĭm ōnce | bĕfōre
> Ās hĕ | pāssĕd | bȳ thĕ | dōor | ănd ă | gāin
> Thĕ pāve | mĕnt stōnes | rĕsōund
> Ās hĕ | tōttĕrs | ō'er thĕ | grōund | wĭth hĭs | cāne.

The pausing or terminating force of the cæsura is
here clearly seen. In the second line, as just remod-
elled, we make a pause in the trochaical rhythms by
means of " door." The " and again " has the air of
a resumption; which in fact it is. The word " passed,"
in the volume from which we extract the poem (**Mr.**
Griswold's *Poets and Poetry of America*) has been
printed with an elision, " pass'd," and thus made one
syllable, but improperly, for each syllable requires
full accentuation to form the trochee.

If we look at the second stanza, we shall perceive
that in the line

> Nŏt ă | bĕttĕr | măn wăs | fōund,

Notes on English Verse

which, according to the construction of the first stanza, should be iambical, the author has merely continued the trochees of the preceding verse. The third stanza is constructed as the second. So also the fourth, with a variation in the line,

> Have been carved for many a year,

which is thus scanned:

> Hāve bĕen | cārv'd fŏr | mănў ă | yĕar.

Here, in place of the expected trochee, we have a dactyl. Referring to the prosodies, we learn that " by a synæresis (blending) of the two short syllables, an anapæst may sometimes be employed for an iambus, or a dactyl for a trochee "; all of which is true, but excessively unsatisfactory. The rationale of the matter is untouched. I was perhaps wrong in admitting even the truth of the rule. The fact is that in cases such as this the synæresis of the syllables is erroneously urged. There should be no blending of the two short syllables into one; and, unquestionably, if blended, the result would be one long, to which they are equivalent; thus the blending would be far from producing a trochee, inasmuch as it would produce more. The idea of the versifier here is discord for the relief of monotone. The time of the pulsation is purposely increased that the ear may not be palled by

297

the too continuous harmony. As in music, so in the rhythm of words, this principle of discord is one of the most important, and, when effectively managed, surprises and delights by its vigorous effects. It seems to be an essential, in these variations, that they be never of diminution. A decrease in the ordinary time of the pulsations should never be attempted; but a fine discord is often effected by mere change of the order of syllables, without increase. In iambic rhythms this change is most usually seen. For example:

Ŏ thŏu, | whătēv | ĕr tī | tlĕ plēase | thĭne ĕar,
Dĕan, Drā | pĭer, Bĭck | ĕrstāff, | ŏr Gūl | lĭvĕr,
Whēthĕr | thŏu chōose | Cĕrvān | tĕs' sē | rĭoŭs āir,
Ŏr lāugh | ănd shāke | ĭn Rā | bĕlăis' ĕa | sў chāir.

Here a trochee forms the first foot of the third line. Discords of excess are observed in the concluding foot of the third verse and in the penultimate of the fourth, where anapæsts take place of iambuses.

These various discords, it will be understood, are efforts for the relief of monotone. These efforts produce fluctuations in the metre; and it often happens that these fluctuations, if not subsequently counterbalanced, affect the ear displeasingly, as do unresolved discords in music. Very generally one discord requires a counterbalance at no great interval. This is a point, however, which only a very nice ear can appreciate. Pope felt its importance, and more especially Milton. I quote an example from the latter:

Notes on English Verse

But say, if our *Deliverer* up to heaven
Must re-ascend, what will betide the few
His faithful, left among the unfaithful herd,
The enemies of truth ? who then shall guide
His people, who defend ? will they not deal
More with his *followers* than with him they dealt ?
Be sure they will, *said the Angel.*

" Said the angel " is here used as a single foot, and counterbalances the two previous discords of excess, italicized. To this practice, on the part of Milton, I especially alluded, when speaking of this poet as surpassing Pope " in the adjusting of his harmonies through paragraphs of greater length than the latter ever ventured to attempt."

Discords of excess are also employed (and even more than one in a line) with the view of equalizing the time of a verse with the real time of a preceding one, when the apparent time of this preceding does not exceed the ordinary rhythm. For example:

But such | a bulk | as no | twelve bards | could raise,
Twelve *starveling* bards of these *degenerate* days.

If we scan the first of these lines we find only the ordinary iambuses; but by the use of unusually long syllables the verse is made to labor in accordance with the author's favorite whim of " making the sound an echo to the sense." It will be found impossible to read aloud

But such a bulk as no twelve bards could raise

Notes on English Verse

in the usual time of five iambuses. The drag of the line, therefore, is properly counterbalanced by two anapæsts in the succeeding; which is thus scanned:

Twĕlve stār | vĕ́lĭng bārds | ĭn thēse | dĕgēn | ĕrătĕ dāys,

Some editions of Pope read, with elision, thus:

Twelve starv'ling bards of these degen'rate days;

but this is, of course, improper. Our books, in general, are full of false elisions.

But to return to our scansion of *The Last Leaf.* The fifth and sixth stanzas exactly resemble the second. The seventh differs from all the others. The second line, as well as the first, is iambic. The whole should be thus divided:

I knōw | ĭt īs | ă sīn | fŏr mē | tŏ sīt | ănd grīn
Āt hĭm | hĕre | būt thĕ | ōld thrĕe | cōrnĕr'd | hăt | ānd
thĕ | brēechĕs | ānd ăll | thāt | āre sŏ | quēer.

In saying that the whole should be thus divided I mean only to say that this is the true grouping of the pulsations; and have no reference to the rhymes. I speak as if these latter had no existence.

The last stanza embraces still another variation. It is entirely trochaic; and involves the only absolute error to be seen in the whole versification. The rhythm requires that the first syllable of the second line should be long; but " the " is a monosyllable which can never be forced, by any accentuation, into length. . . .

Notes on English Verse

In truth, from the character of its terminations (most frequently in " um, am, i, o, os," etc.), as well as from the paucity of the monosyllabic articles and pronouns so prevalent in the Saxon, the Latin is a far more stately tongue than our own. It is essentially spondaic; the English is as essentially dactylic. The long syllable is the spirit of the Roman (and Greek) verse; the short syllable is the essence of ours. In casting the eye, for example, over the lines of Silius . . . we shall not fail to perceive the great preponderance of the spondee [1]; and, in examining the so-called hexameters . . . by Professor Longfellow, we shall, in the same manner, see the predominance of the dactyl. English hexameters are always about one third longer to the eye than Latin or Greek ones. Now it follows, from what has been here explained, that English hexameters are radically different from Latin ones: for it is the predominant foot, or pulsation, which gives the tone to the verse or establishes its rhythm. Latin hexameters are spondaic rhythms, varied by equivalent dactyls. English hexameters are dactylic rhythms, varied, rarely, by equivalent spondees. Not that we cannot have English hexameters, in every respect correspondent to the Latin; but that such can be constructed only by a minuteness of labor, and with a forced or far-fetched appearance, which

---

[1] Even the regula. dactyl in the penultimate foot is often displaced by a spondee in Latin hexam. ~s.

Notes on English Verse

are at war with their employment to any extent. In building them we must search for spondaic words, which, in English, are rare indeed; or, in their default, we must construct spondees of long monosyllables, although the majority of our monosyllables are short. I quote here an unintentional instance of a perfect English hexameter formed upon the model of the Greek:

Man is a complex, compound, compost, yet is he God-born.

This line is thus scanned:

Mān ĭs ă | cōmplēx | cōmpŏund | cōmpŏst | yĕt ĭs hĕ | Gŏd-bōrn.

I say that this is " a perfect English hexameter formed upon the model of the Greek," because, while its rhythm is plainly spondaic varied by dactyls, and thus is essentially Greek (or Latin), it yet preserves, as all English verse should preserve, a concordance between its scansion and reading-flow. Such lines, of course, cannot be composed without a degree of difficulty which must effect their exclusion, for all practical purposes, from our tongue. . . .

Whatever defects may be found in the harmony of our poets, their errors of melody are still more conspicuous. Here the field is, comparatively, one of little extent. The versifier who is at all aware of the nature of the rhythms with which he is engaged, can scarcely err, in melody, unless through carelessness or affectation. The rules for his guidance are simple and few. He should employ his syllables, as nearly as possible, with the accentuation due in prose reading. His short syllables should never be encumbered with many consonants, and, especially, never with those difficult of pronunciation. His long syllables should depend as much as possible upon full vowels or diphthongal sounds for length. His periods, or equivalent pauses, should not be so placed as to interrupt a rhythm. Further than this, little need be said. It is therefore justly matter for surprise, when we meet, amid the iambics of so fine a versifier as Mr. Bryant, for example, such lines as,

Languished in the damp shade and died afar from men;

or, still worse, as,

Kind influence. Lo, their orbs burn more bright;

in the latter of which we can preserve the metre only by drawing out " influence " into three strongly marked syllables, shortening the long monosyllable " Lo," and lengthening the short one, " their."

In turning over a poem by Alfred B. Street, my attention is arrested by these lines:

Hĭs sīn | ŭoŭs pāth, | bў̆ blā | zĕs, wōund
Ă̆mōng | trŭnks groūp'd | ĭn mȳ- | rĭ̆ăds rōund.

Every reader will here perceive the impossibility of pronouncing " trunks " as a short syllable. The difficulty arises from the number of harsh consonants by which the vowel " u " is surrounded. There is a rule in Latin prosody that a vowel before two consonants is long. We moderns have not only no such rule, but profess inability to comprehend its rationale. If, nevertheless, from the natural limit to man's power of syllabification, a vowel before two consonants is inevitably long, how shall we properly understand as short one which is embedded among nine ? Yet Mr. Street is one of our finest versifiers, and his error is but one of a class in which all his brethren most pertinaciously indulge.

But I must bring this paper to a close. It will not be supposed that my object has been a treatise upon verse. A world more than I have room to say might be said. I have endeavored to deal with principles while seeming busy with details. A right application of these principles will clear up much obscurity in our common acceptation of rhythm; but, throughout, it has been my design not so much thoroughly to investigate the topic as to dwell upon those salient points of it which have been either totally neglected or inefficiently discussed.

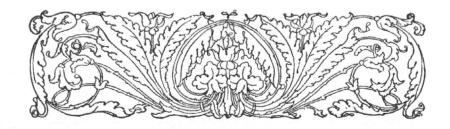

The Philosophy of Composition.

CHARLES DICKENS, in a note now lying before me, alluding to an examination I once made of the mechanism of *Barnaby Rudge,* says: " By the way, are you aware that Godwin wrote his *Caleb Williams* backward ? He first involved his hero in a web of difficulties, forming the second volume, and then, for the first, cast about him for some mode of accounting for what had been done."

I cannot think this the precise mode of procedure on the part of Godwin, and indeed what he himself acknowledges is not altogether in accordance with Mr. Dickens's idea; but the author of *Caleb Williams* was too good an artist not to perceive the advantage derivable from at least a somewhat similar process. Nothing is more clear than that every plot, worth the name, must be elaborated to its *dénouement* before anything be attempted with the pen. It is only with the *dénouement* constantly in view that we can give a plot its

The Philosophy of Composition

indispensable air of consequence, or causation, by making the incidents, and especially the tone at all points, tend to the development of the intention.

There is a radical error, I think, in the usual mode of constructing a story. Either history affords a thesis, or one is suggested by an incident of the day, or, at best, the author sets himself to work in the combination of striking events to form merely the basis of his narrative, designing, generally, to fill in with description, dialogue, or authorial comment, whatever crevices of fact or action may, from page to page, render themselves apparent.

I prefer commencing with the consideration of an effect. Keeping originality always in view,—for he is false to himself who ventures to dispense with so obvious and so easily attainable a source of interest,—I say to myself, in the first place: " Of the innumerable effects, or impressions, of which the heart, the intellect, or (more generally) the soul is susceptible, what one shall I, on the present occasion, select ? " Having chosen a novel, first, and secondly a vivid effect, I consider whether it can be best wrought by incident or tone,—whether by ordinary incidents and peculiar tone, or the converse, or by peculiarity both of incident and tone; afterward looking about me, or rather within, for such combinations of event, or tone, as shall best aid me in the construction of the effect.

I have often thought how interesting a magazine

The Philosophy of Composition

paper might be written by any author who would, that is to say, who could, detail, step by step, the processes by which any one of his compositions attained its ultimate point of completion. Why such a paper has never been given to the world I am much at a loss to say, but perhaps the authorial vanity has had more to do with the omission than any one other cause. Most writers, poets in especial, prefer having it understood that they compose by a species of fine frenzy, an ecstatic intuition, and would positively shudder at letting the public take a peep behind the scenes at the elaborate and vacillating crudities of thought; at the true purposes seized only at the last moment; at the innumerable glimpses of idea that arrived not at the maturity of full view; at the fully matured fancies discarded in despair as unmanageable; at the cautious selections and rejections; at the painful erasures and interpolations,—in a word, at the wheels and pinions, the tackle for scene-shifting, the step-ladders and demon-traps, the cock's feathers, the red paint and the black patches which, in ninety-nine cases out of the hundred, constitute the properties of the literary histrio.

I am aware, on the other hand, that the case is by no means common in which an author is at all in condition to retrace the steps by which his conclusions have been attained. In general, suggestions, having arisen pell-mell, are pursued and forgotten in a similar manner.

The Philosophy of Composition

For my own part, I have neither sympathy with the repugnance alluded to, nor, at any time, the least difficulty in recalling to mind the progressive steps of any of my compositions; and, since the interest of an analysis, or reconstruction, such as I have considered a desideratum, is quite independent of any real or fancied interest in the thing analyzed, it will not be regarded as a breach of decorum on my part to show the *modus operandi* by which some one of my own works was put together. I select *The Raven* as most generally known. It is my design to render it manifest that no one point in its composition is referable either to accident or intuition, that the work proceeded, step by step, to its completion with the precision and rigid consequence of a mathematical problem.

Let us dismiss, as irrelevant to the poem *per se,* the circumstance, or say the necessity, which, in the first place, gave rise to the intention of composing a poem that should suit at once the popular and the critical taste.

We commence, then, with this intention.

The initial consideration was that of extent. If any literary work is too long to be read at one sitting, we must be content to dispense with the immensely important effect derivable from unity of impression; for, if two sittings be required, the affairs of the world interfere, and everything like totality is at once destroyed. But since, *ceteris paribus,* no poet can afford

The Philosophy of Composition

to dispense with anything that may advance his design, it but remains to be seen whether there is, in extent, any advantage to counterbalance the loss of unity which attends it. Here I say no, at once. What we term a long poem is, in fact, merely a succession of brief ones; that is to say, of brief poetical effects. It is needless to demonstrate that a poem is such, only inasmuch as it intensely excites, by elevating, the soul; and all intense excitements are, through a physical necessity, brief. For this reason, at least one half of the *Paradise Lost* is essentially prose, a succession of poetical excitements interspersed, inevitably, with corresponding depressions, the whole being deprived, through the extremeness of its length, of the vastly important artistic element, totality, or unity, of effect.

It appears evident, then, that there is a distinct limit, as regards length, to all works of literary art—the limit of a single sitting—and that, although in certain classes of prose composition, such as *Robinson Crusoe* (demanding no unity), this limit may be advantageously overpassed, it can never properly be overpassed in a poem. Within this limit, the extent of a poem may be made to bear mathematical relation to its merit; in other words, to the excitement or elevation; again, in other words, to the degree of the true poetical effect which it is capable of inducing; for it is clear that the brevity must be in direct ratio of the intensity of the intended effect:—this, with one proviso, that a certain degree of duration is absolutely requisite for the production of any effect at all.

Holding in view these considerations, as well as that degree of excitement which I deemed not above the popular, while not below the critical, taste, I reached at once what I conceived the proper length for my intended poem, a length of about one hundred lines. It is, in fact, a hundred and eight.

My next thought concerned the choice of an impression, or effect, to be conveyed; and here I may as well observe that, throughout the construction, I kept steadily in view the design of rendering the work universally appreciable. I should be carried too far out of my immediate topic were I to demonstrate a point upon which I have repeatedly insisted, and which, with the poetical, stands not in the slightest need of demonstration—the point, I mean, that beauty is the sole legitimate province of the poem. A few words, however, in elucidation of my real meaning, which some of my friends have evinced a disposition to misrepresent. That pleasure which is at once the most intense, the most elevating, and the most pure, is, I believe, found in the contemplation of the beautiful. When, indeed, men speak of beauty, they mean, precisely, not a quality, as is supposed, but an effect; they refer, in short, just to that intense and pure elevation of soul, not of intellect or of heart, upon which I have commented, and which is experienced in consequence of

The Philosophy of Composition

contemplating " the beautiful." Now I designate beauty as the province of the poem, merely because it is an obvious rule of art that effects should be made to spring from direct causes, that objects should be attained through means best adapted for their attainment, no one as yet having been weak enough to deny that the peculiar elevation alluded to is most readliy attained in the poem. Now the object, truth, or the satisfaction of the intellect, and the object, passion, or the excitement of the heart, are, although attainable to a certain extent in poetry, far more readily attainable in prose. Truth, in fact, demands a precision, and passion a homeliness (the truly passionate will comprehend me), which are absolutely antagonistic to that beauty which, I maintain, is the excitement, or pleasurable elevation, of the soul. It by no means follows from anything here said, that passion, or even truth, may not be introduced, and even profitably introduced, into a poem, for they may serve in elucidation, or aid the general effect, as do discords in music, by contrast; but the true artist will always contrive, first, to tone them into proper subservience to the predominant aim, and, secondly, to enveil them, as far as possible, in that beauty which is the atmosphere and the essence of the poem.

Regarding, then, beauty as my province, my next question referred to the tone of its highest manifestation, and all experience has shown that this tone is

The Philosophy of Composition

one of sadness. Beauty of whatever kind, in its supreme development, invariably excites the sensitive soul to tears. Melancholy is thus the most legitimate of all the poetical tones.

The length, the province, and the tone, being thus determined, I betook myself to ordinary induction, with the view of obtaining some artistic piquancy which might serve me as a key-note in the construction of the poem, some pivot upon which the whole structure might turn. In carefully thinking over all the usual artistic effects, or, more properly, points, in the theatrical sense, I did not fail to perceive immediately that no one had been so universally employed as that of the refrain. The universality of its employment sufficed to assure me of its intrinsic value, and spared me the necessity of submitting it to analysis. I considered it, however, with regard to its susceptibility of improvement, and soon saw it to be in a primitive condition. As commonly used, the refrain, or burden, not only is limited to lyric verse, but depends for its impression upon the force of monotone, both in sound and thought. The pleasure is deduced solely from the sense of identity—of repetition. I resolved to diversity, and so heighten, the effect, by adhering, in general, to the monotone of sound, while I continually varied that of thought : that is to say, I determined to produce continuously novel effects, by the variation of the application of the refrain, the refrain itself remaining, for the most part, unvaried.

These points being settled, I next bethought me of the nature of my refrain. Since its application was to be repeatedly varied, it was clear that the refrain itself must be brief, for there would have been an insurmountable difficulty in frequent variations of application in any sentence of length. In proportion to the brevity of the sentence, would, of course, be the facility of the variation. This led me at once to a single word as the best refrain.

The question now arose as to the character of the word. Having made up my mind to a refrain, the division of the poem into stanzas was, of course, a corollary, the refrain forming the close to each stanza. That such a close, to have force, must be sonorous and susceptible of protracted emphasis admitted no doubt; and these considerations inevitably led me to the long " o " as the most sonorous vowel, in connection with " r " as the most producible consonant.

The sound of the refrain being thus determined, it became necessary to select a word embodying this sound, and at the same time in the fullest possible keeping with that melancholy which I had predetermined as the tone of the poem. In such a search it would have been absolutely impossible to overlook the word " Nevermore." In fact, it was the very first which presented itself.

The Philosophy of Composition

The next desideratum was a pretext for the continuous use of the one word " Nevermore." In observing the difficulty which I at once found in inventing a sufficiently plausible reason for its continuous repetition, I did not fail to perceive that this difficulty arose solely from the pre-assumption that the word was to be so continuously or monotonously spoken by a human being; I did not fail to perceive, in short, that the difficulty lay in the reconciliation of this monotony with the exercise of reason on the part of the creature repeating the word. Here, then, immediately arose the idea of a non-reasoning creature capable of speech; and, very naturally, a parrot, in the first instance, suggested itself, but was superseded forthwith by a Raven, as equally capable of speech, and infinitely more in keeping with the intended tone.

I had now gone so far as the conception of a Raven, the bird of ill omen, monotonously repeating the one word, " Nevermore," at the conclusion of each stanza, in a poem of melancholy tone, and in length about one hundred lines. Now, never losing sight of the object, supremeness, or perfection, at all points, I asked myself: " Of all melancholy topics, what, according to the universal understanding of mankind, is the most melancholy ? " " Death " was the obvious reply. " And when," I said, " is this most melancholy of topics most poetical ? " From what I have already explained at some length, the answer here, also, is obvious: " When it most closely allies itself to beauty: the death, then, of a beautiful woman is, unquestionably, the most poetical topic in the world; and equally is it beyond doubt that the lips best suited for such topic are those of a bereaved lover."

I had now to combine the two ideas, of a lover lamenting his deceased mistress and a Raven continuously repeating the word " Nevermore." I had to combine these, bearing in mind my design of varying, at every turn, the application of the word repeated; but the only intelligible mode of such combination is that of imagining the Raven employing the word in answer to the queries of the lover. And here it was that I saw at once the opportunity afforded for the effect on which I had been depending; that is to say, the effect of the variation of application. I saw that I could make the first query propounded by the lover the first query to which the Raven should reply " Nevermore," that I could make this first query a commonplace one; the second less so, the third still less, and so on, until at length the lover, startled from his original nonchalance by the melancholy character of the word itself, by its frequent repetition, and by a consideration of the ominous reputation of the fowl that uttered it, is at length excited to superstition, and wildly propounds queries of a far different character, —queries whose solution he has passionately at heart, —propounds them half in superstition and half in

that species of despair which delights in self-torture;
propounds them not altogether because he believes in
the prophetic or demoniac character of the bird (which,
reason assures him, is merely repeating a lesson
learned by rote), but because he experiences a frenzied
pleasure in so modelling his questions as to receive
from the expected " Nevermore " the most delicious
because the most intolerable of sorrow. Perceiving
the opportunity thus afforded me, or, more strictly,
thus forced upon me in the progress of the construc-
tion, I first established in mind the climax, or conclud-
ing query—that query to which " Nevermore " should
be in the last place an answer; that query in reply to
which this word " Nevermore " should involve the
utmost conceivable amount of sorrow and despair.

Here, then, the poem may be said to have its begin-
ning—at the end, where all works of art should begin;
for it was here, at this point of my preconsiderations,
that I first put pen to paper in the composition of the
stanza:

"Prophet," said I, "thing of evil! prophet still, if bird or
    devil!
By that heaven that bends above us, by that God we both
    adore,
Tell this soul with sorrow laden if, within the distant Aidenn,
It shall clasp a sainted maiden whom the angels name Lenore,
Clasp a rare and radiant maiden whom the angels name
    Lenore."
                    Quoth the Raven, " Nevermore."

The Philosophy of Composition

I composed this stanza, at this point, first that, by establishing the climax, I might the better vary and graduate, as regards seriousness and importance, the preceding queries of the lover; and, secondly, that I might definitely settle the rhythm, the metre, and the length and general arrangement of the stanzas, as well as graduate the stanzas which were to precede, so that none of them might surpass this in rhythmical effect. Had I been able, in the subsequent composition, to construct more vigorous stanzas, I should, without scruple, have purposely enfeebled them, so as not to interfere with the climacteric effect.

And here I may as well say a few words of the versification. My first object, as usual, was originality. The extent to which this has been neglected in versification is one of the most unaccountable things in the world. Admitting that there is little possibility of variety in mere rhythm, it is still clear that the possible varieties of metre and stanza are absolutely infinite; and yet, for centuries, no man, in verse, has ever done, or ever seemed to think of doing, an original thing. The fact is, that originality, unless in minds of very unusual force, is by no means a matter, as some suppose, of impulse or intuition. In general, to be found, it must be elaborately sought, and although a positive merit of the highest class, demands in its attainment less of invention than negation.

Of course, I pretend to no originality in either the

rhythm or metre of *The Raven.* The former is tro-
chaic; the latter is octameter acatalectic, alternating
with heptameter catalectic repeated in the refrain of
the fifth verse, and terminating with tetrameter cata-
lectic. Less pedantically, the feet employed through-
out (trochees) consist of a long syllable followed by a
short: the first line of the stanza consists of eight of
these feet; the second of seven and a half (in effect
two thirds); the third of eight; the fourth of seven and
a half; the fifth the same; the sixth three and a half.
Now, each of these lines, taken individually, has been
employed before, and what originality *The Raven* has,
is in their combination into stanza; nothing even
remotely approaching this combination has ever been
attempted. The effect of this originality of combina-
tion is aided by other unusual and some altogether
novel effects, arising from an extension of the applica-
tion of the principles of rhyme and alliteration.

The next point to be considered was the mode of
bringing together the lover and the Raven, and the first
branch of this consideration was the locale. For this
the most natural suggestion might seem to be a forest
or the fields, but it has always appeared to me that a
close circumscription of space is absolutely necessary
to the effect of insulated incident: it has the force of a
frame to a picture. It has an indisputable moral power
in keeping concentrated the attention, and, of course,
must not be confounded with mere unity of place.

The Philosophy of Composition

I determined, then, to place the lover in his chamber,—in a chamber rendered sacred to him by memories of her who had frequented it. The room is represented as richly furnished; this, in mere pursuance of the ideas I have already explained on the subject of beauty as the sole true poetical thesis.

The locale being thus determined, I had now to introduce the bird, and the thought of introducing him through the window was inevitable. The idea of making the lover suppose, in the first instance, that the flapping of the wings of the bird against the shutter is a " tapping " at the door originated in a wish to increase, by prolonging, the reader's curiosity, and in a desire to admit the incidental effect arising from the lover's throwing open the door, finding all dark, and thence adopting the half-fancy that it was the spirit of his mistress that knocked.

I made the night tempestuous, first, to account for the Raven's seeking admission, and, secondly, for the effect of contrast with the physical serenity within the chamber.

I made the bird alight on the bust of Pallas, also for the effect of contrast between the marble and the plumage,—it being understood that the bust was absolutely suggested by the bird; the bust of Pallas being chosen, first, as most in keeping with the scholarship of the lover, and, secondly, for the sonorousness of the word " Pallas " itself.

The Philosophy of Composition

About the middle of the poem, also, I have availed myself of the force of contrast, with a view of deepening the ultimate impression. For example, an air of the fantastic, approaching as nearly to the ludicrous as was admissible, is given to the Raven's entrance. He comes in " with many a flirt and flutter."

Not the *least obeisance made he;* not a moment stopped or stayed he,
But with mien of lord or lady, perched above my chamber door.

In the two stanzas which follow, the design is more obviously carried out:

Then this ebony bird beguiling my sad fancy into smiling,
By the *grave and stern decorum of the countenance it wore,*
" Though thy *crest be shorn and shaven,* thou," I said, "art sure no craven,
Ghastly grim and ancient Raven wandering from the nightly shore;
Tell me what thy lordly name is on the Night's Plutonian shore ? "
　　　　　　　　　Quoth the Raven, " Nevermore."

Much I marvelled *this ungainly fowl* to hear discourse so plainly,
Though its answer little meaning, little relevancy bore;
For we cannot help agreeing that no living human being
Ever yet was blest with seeing bird above his chamber door—
Bird or beast upon the sculptured bust above his chamber door,
　　　　　　　　　With such name as " Nevermore."

The effect of the *dénouement* being thus provided for, I immediately drop the fantastic for a tone of the most profound seriousness, this tone commencing in the stanza directly following the one last quoted, with the line,

But the Raven, sitting lonely on that placid bust, spoke only,
etc.

From this epoch the lover no longer jests, no longer sees anything even of the fantastic in the Raven's demeanor. He speaks of him as a " grim, ungainly, ghastly, gaunt, and ominous bird of yore," and feels the " fiery eyes " burning into his " bosom's core." This revolution of thought, or fancy, on the lover's part is intended to induce a similar one on the part of the reader—to bring the mind into a proper frame for the *dénouement* which is now brought about as rapidly and as directly as possible.

With the *dénouement* proper—with the Raven's reply, " Nevermore," to the lover's final demand if he shall meet his mistress in another world, the poem, in its obvious phase, that of a single narrative, may be said to have its completion. So far, everything is within the limits of the accountable, of the real. A Raven, having learned by rote the single word, " Nevermore," and having escaped from the custody of its owner, is driven at midnight, through the violence of a storm, to seek admission at a window from which a light still gleams,—the chamber-window of a student, occupied half in poring over a volume, half in dreaming over a beloved mistress deceased. The casement being thrown open at the fluttering of a bird's wings, the bird itself perches on the most convenient seat out of the immediate reach of the student, who, amused by the incident and the oddity of the visitor's demeanor, demands of it, in jest and without looking for a reply, its name. The Raven, addressed, answers with its customary word, " Nevermore," a word which finds immediate echo in the melancholy heart of the student, who, giving utterance aloud to certain thoughts suggested by the occasion, is again startled by the fowl's repetition of " Nevermore." The student now guesses the state of the case, but is impelled, as I have before explained, by the human thirst for self-torture, and in part by superstition, to propound such queries to the bird as will bring him, the lover, the most of the luxury of sorrow, through the anticipated answer, " Nevermore." With the indulgence, to the extreme, of this self-torture, the narration, in what I have termed its first or obvious phase, has a natural termination, and so far there has been no overstepping of the limits of the real.

But in subjects so handled, however skilfully, or with however vivid an array of incident, there is always a certain hardness or nakedness, which repels the artistical eye. Two things are invariably required: first, some amount of complexity, or more properly, adaptation; and, secondly, some amount of suggestiveness, some undercurrent, however indefinite, of meaning. It is this latter, in especial, which imparts to a work of art so much of that richness (to borrow from colloquy a forcible term) which we are too fond of confounding with the ideal. It is the excess of the suggested meaning, it is the rendering this the upper- instead of the under-current of the theme, which turns into prose (and that of the very flattest kind) the so-called poetry of the so-called transcendentalists.

Holding these opinions, I added the two concluding stanzas of the poem, their suggestiveness being thus made to pervade all the narrative which has preceded them. The under-current of meaning is rendered first apparent in the lines,

"Take thy beak from out *my heart,* and take thy form from
    off my door ! "

                Quoth the Raven, " Nevermore ! "

It will be observed that the words, " from out my heart," involve the first metaphorical expression in the poem. They, with the answer, " Nevermore," dispose the mind to seek a moral in all that has been previously narrated. The reader begins now to regard the Raven as emblematical, but it is not until the very last line of the very last stanza that the intention of making him emblematical of mournful and never-ending remembrance is permitted distinctly to be seen:

VOL. I.—20.

The Philosophy of Composition

And the Raven, never flitting, still is sitting, still is sitting
On the pallid bust of Pallas just above my chamber door;
And his eyes have all the seeming of a demon's that is dream-
   ing,
And the lamplight o'er him streaming throws his shadow on
   the floor;
And my soul *from out that shadow* that lies floating on the
   floor

                  Shall be lifted—nevermore.

Edgar Allan Poe, World-Author

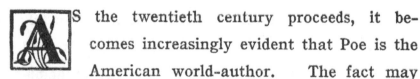

S the twentieth century proceeds, it becomes increasingly evident that Poe is the American world-author. The fact may be received with acclamation or regret, willingly or grudgingly, but it remains.

Matthew Arnold once remarked that the United States ought to cease talking about a national literature, and produce, if possible, an occasional Franklin or Grant. But the fame of Lincoln now overshadows that of his chief general, and neither the President nor the soldier, of course, addresses the public of readers for his chief renown. Franklin was a mighty force in his day, more widely influential than

Edgar Allan Poe

any of his colonial contemporaries; but Mr. Arnold would hardly have claimed a high literary place for the aphorisms of *Poor Richard* or the simple honesty of the *Autobiography.* Indeed, the very point made by the English critic was that America might produce men of affairs but not creative artists.

One is very ready to admit this statement as regards our writers before Irving. Even in the realm of theology, and the related division of spiritual philosophy, the New England of the seventeenth and eighteenth centuries made no addition to permanent literature, though the definition of that term be stretched beyond reason. The name of Jonathan Edwards stands high among those who no longer read him, but who declare him a master of invincible logic because of his argument that one cannot decide until he decides to decide. Mere literature was more nearly approached in the writings of Increase Mather than in those of his more famous contemporary. The student of the development of creative genius turns coolly aside from the preacher or the patriot, and takes pleasure in some little foregleam of Poe in the writings of Brockden Brown, whom Shelley admired. A single line in Philip Freneau's *The House of Night,*

X

326

EDGAR ALLAN POE
Etched by T. Johnson from a daguerreotype.

World-Author

Trim the dull tapers, for I see no dawn,

would not be exchanged by the poetry-lover for the
whole of one of those *Complete Bodies of Divinity*
with which the Boston divines burdened the world.

When the name of Poe is set against those of the
chief American writers of his own time a different
competition is suggested. To Emerson Poe seemed a
" jingle man," and it must certainly be admitted, as
a truism, that in the prose and verse of Emerson there
is a high acquiescence, a noble optimism, a stimulating
intellectual independence, which his fellow-native of
Boston could never show. But while most of the
doctrine of Emerson may be found elsewhere, from
Plato to Browning, Poe is unique. No one, I suppose,
would seriously think of ranking Whittier, Lowell, or
Holmes with either of these two; but we cannot deny
the fact that to many the gentle and somewhat
obvious didacticism of Longfellow, expressed as it is,
in measures of Heine-like mellifluousness, appears of
greater beauty than Poe's " hollow tintinnabulations."
It may not prove a rash prophecy, however, that of
all Longfellow's writings *Hiawatha,* because the most
characteristic and indigenous, will be the last to
perish. As regards the general field of American
poetry, a recent English critic has declared, with that

xi

accurate nicety of self-confidence which sometimes distinguishes his guild, that America has thus far produced exactly a poet and a half,—that is to say, Poe in both thought and form, Whitman in thought but not in form.

It is interesting to note the incisive criticism which the half-poet made of the whole-poet. Said Whitman, in an informal circle in Baltimore, at the time of what he called the " public reburial of Poe's remains " in 1875: " For a long while, and until lately, I had a distaste for Poe's writings. I wanted, and still want for poetry, the clear sun shining and fresh air blowing —the strength and power of health, not of delirium, even amid the stormiest passions—with always the background of the eternal moralities. Non-complying with these requirements, Poe's genius has yet conquered a special recognition for itself, and I too have come to fully admit it, and appreciate it and him." Five years later, in an article (including the above) on " Edgar Poe's Significance," Whitman gave the following concise and certainly noteworthy estimate of his famous predecessor and counterpart: " Almost without the first sign of moral principle, or of the concrete or its heroisms, or the simpler affections of the heart, Poe's verses illustrate an intense faculty for

xii

technical and abstract beauty, with the rhyming art to excess, an incorrigible propensity toward nocturnal themes, a demoniac undertone behind every page; and, by final judgment, probably belong among the electric lights of imaginative literature, brilliant and dazzling, but with no heat."

Between Whitman and Poe there can be no comparison whatever; it is enough to say, as regards the matter of world-literature, that the earnest admiration shown for Whitman in England, Italy, and elsewhere, as the utter American, forms no offset to the eager and widespread acclaim accorded Poe. Even in the matter of absolute originality of idea and expression Poe equals Whitman, and his message of beauty and immortal individualism is not less cogent than Whitman's of comradeship and courage.

In estimating the rank of Poe or any other author we are of course brought quickly back to questions of terms. If we mean ethics we mean one thing, if art, another. The everlasting discussion narrows itself, sooner or later, to the statement that, other things being equal, the great artists of the world, in any field, have joined moral perception to the perception of beauty of form. There is one American author who, in my opinion, ought to outrank Poe, even when submitted

to the same comparative tests. Is Poe a man of un-
questionable and original genius?—so is Hawthorne,
though Poe himself thought not. Are his creations
so new, is his style so much his own, is his field so
nearly unexploited by others, that everybody knows the
meaning of the word "Poesque"? "Hawthornesque"
has in our vocabularies a place not less clearly its own.
Indeed, *The Devil in Manuscript* might have been
one of the *Tales Grotesque and Arabesque* and *The
Man of the Crowd* have been included in *Mosses from
an Old Manse.* Was Poe the "poet of weird woe"?
Hawthorne has always seemed "morbid" to the
careless reader; even Emerson said that he rode
well his steed of the night, and Whittier seems
to have regarded him as a sort of miserable New
England Poe: "And so Hawthorne is at rest, the rest
that he could not find here. God, the all-merciful,
has removed him from the shadows of time, wherein
he seemed to walk, himself a shadow, to the clear
sunlight of eternity." All of which shows that to be
a noted author is not necessarily to be a sage critic.
If Poe sometimes moved in the ghoul-haunted wood-
land of Weir, and Hawthorne in the depths of the sin-
stained soul, each—in *William Wilson* and in *Ethan
Brand,* respectively—wrote a little bible of the moral

xiv

life. For the rest, *suum cuique;* it is enough to say that in many of his most characteristic powers of creation and expression Poe finds a noteworthy fellow in that great New England writer whom he misjudged in some ways, but declared to have " the purest style, the finest taste, the most available scholarship, the most delicate humor, the most touching pathos, the most radiant imagination, the most consummate ingenuity "; and that to some of us, in these latter years, it appears that Hawthorne's view of the material and spiritual universe is both broader and deeper than Poe's, and that, with the important reservation that he wrote only in prose, he ought to be esteemed the higher of the two.

But the world and the years are the obvious arbiters of fame, and in the half-century since the death of our chief creative geniuses the general vote has been given to the singer of *The Raven* and the teller of the tale of *Ligeia.* Said Tennyson: " I know several striking poems by American poets, but I think that Edgar Poe is (taking his poetry and prose together) the most original American genius." When asked to write an epitaph of one line for Poe's monument in Westminster churchyard, Baltimore, he answered: " How can so strange and so fine a genius, and so sad a life, be exprest and comprest in one line?" To Victor Hugo, Poe was the "prince of American literature." "Widely as the fame of Poe has already spread"—says the author of *Atalanta in Calydon* and *A Forsaken Garden*—"and deeply as it is already rooted in Europe, it is even now growing wider and striking deeper as time advances." To the inspiration of *The Raven* we owe what in some ways is the most original poem since written: Rossetti's *The Blessed Damozel.* Rossetti told Hall Caine, in 1881, that the latter ballad grew out of his love for the former while still a boy: "I saw that Poe had done the utmost it was possible to do with the grief of the lover on earth; and so I determined to reverse the conditions, and give utterance to the yearning of the loved one in heaven." Mr. William Michael Rossetti testifies that he can recollect his brother's bringing home some cheap English magazine containing a re-print of *The Raven* and the zest with which he read it over and over again to his family of poets. To Poe's most industrious and enthusiastic English editor, *The Raven* appears "the most popular lyrical poem in the world. It has been translated and commented upon by the leading literati of two continents, and an entire literature has been founded upon it."

xvi

World-Author

These opinions of earnest advocates are paralleled by the sober tabulation of the publishers' lists. Taking five representative libraries of world-literature, in English, German, and Italian, Poe's is the only name appearing in all five. In France his fame is greater than that of any other American writer, or than that of most English writers, and he has influenced an entire school of Parisian *poètes d'aujourd'hui.* In many a little German, Austrian, or Italian bookshop he stands as the sole representative of the literature of his native land. Forty years ago a French critic made his name the synonym for originality, which he neatly defined as *l'affirmation de l'indépendance individuelle ; c'est le* " self-government " *appliqué aux œuvres d'art.* " Certain things," said an Italian writer in *Il Marzocco* the other day, "can only have been written by Poe, by Heine, by Tolstoi; one does not need to see the cover of the book,—read it, and the name of the author will come spontaneously to the lips." The most violent and independent of contemporary English critics makes the author of *Annabel Lee* his final name in a collection of lyrics bearing, as its significant subtitle, *Chaucer to Poe,* and in his preface he makes this comprehensive claim: " After Keats there is no fresh note, until we hear from

Edgar Allan Poe

over the Atlantic the artful, subtle, irresistible song of Poe: the new music which none that has heard it can forget, and which, if you listen for it, you will catch in much of the melody that has found utterance since Mr. Swinburne, working after Baudelaire, shocked and enchanted the world with his first series of *Poems and Ballads."*

A serious mistake, which has grown current by mere thoughtless iteration, is that Poe has always been unappreciated in his own country. This fallacy exists chiefly, perhaps, in France, whose writers have deemed it their special mission to champion his cause in the face of stolid Anglo-Saxon indifference to the nature of true poetic genius. Baudelaire, writing only three years after Poe's death, said: " Les divers documents que je viens de lire ont créé en moi cette persuasion que les États-Unis furent pour Poe une vaste cage, un grand établissement de comptabilité; et qu'il fit toute sa vie de sinistres efforts pour échapper à l'influence de cette atmosphère antipathique." [1] M. J. H. Rosny, in his introduction to an edition of *The Gold Bug* in French, coolly observes that though Poe was endowed with one of the most powerful original geniuses known in literature, his reputation was but

[1] *Revue de Paris, 1852.*

poor in America; to France has he owed any appreciation at his true worth. M. Camille Mauclair, in his original essay on *Edgar Poe, Idéologue,* declares that Poe was a literary and mental phenomenon, spontaneously shooting up in an ungrateful land, and borne over seas, " between Emerson the sympathetic and Whitman the prophetic, as an interrogator of the future." That there has not been, in America, uniform agreement as to the poet's merits or rank is indisputable; but no American criticism, by Griswold or anybody else, ever equalled the bitterness of some foreign animadversions. It will hardly be believed that the *Edinburgh Review* (April, 1858) used such language as this: " Edgar Allan Poe was incontestably one of the most worthless persons of whom we have any record in the world of letters. Many authors may have been as idle, many as improvident, some as drunken and dissipated, and a few, perhaps, as treacherous and ungrateful; but he seems to have succeeded in attracting and combining, in his own person, all the floating vices which genius had hitherto shown itself capable of grasping in its widest and most eccentric orbit. . . . The weakness of human nature has, we imagine, its limit; but the biography of Poe has satisfied us that the lowest abyss of moral imbecility

xix

and disrepute was never attained until he came, and stood forth a warning for the times to come." Over against this, at the farthest extreme, may be set a recent expression by an Italian enthusiast to the effect that Poe was sent by God as a celestial messenger to earthborn toilers in the shadow.[1]

Mr. Henry James's alliterative characterization of Poe's poems as " very valueless verses " is remembered; but none of Poe's countrymen, as far as I know, ever declared his verse diffuse, tiresome, absurd, nonsense, insanity, as Keats's poems seemed to John Wilson Croker. Poe himself frankly and justly called his earliest writings " trash," at least in part; but similar explicitness is hardly to be found in the comments of his contemporaries. In the thirty-three volumes of histories of American literature, large and small, published since 1829, Poe occupies as high and honorable a place, on the whole, as he deserves. That his catholic importance was not at once perceived was inevitable; but it is idle to speak of him as obscure, unappreciated, or generally decried

---

[1] Adoratore della bellezza nella quale egli ritrovava piacere, tristezza, malinconia, lacrime e consolo a tutte le sue afflizioni, egli apparve come il ' genio del terrore,' mandato da Dio da le celesti sfere, perchè egli parlava linguaggio celestale e sublime, per rivelare agli uomini sulla terra, la virtù dell' orribile ' e del ' terribile ' sotto tutti i suoi aspetti ed in forma e concezione altissima quanto il luogo superiore, dal quale l'anima sua era discesa.''
Dr. Ulisse Ortensi, in la Tavola Rotonda, Naples, Dec. 9, 1900.

XX

in his native land. The rarer and finer natures must blush unseen for a time; the young Hawthorne once called himself the obscurest man of letters in America; but in his day Poe was widely famous, and his renown has broadened ever since. Indeed, his celebrity has been doubled among the multitudes who appreciate the obvious tone pictures of *The Bells* and in the minds of the selecter few who prize such a flawless lyric as the shorter poem *To Helen.* " Byron to the multitude, Edgar Poe to the select," exclaims one of his admirers; but Poe's achievement is to address the mass by *The Raven* and *The Black Cat* while the " remnant " ponders over *Ulalume* or *William Wilson.* " During this winter of 1845," says the late Mr. Scudder, in his life of Lowell " Poe was a lively subject of discussion by Lowell and his friends, for he was the most conspicuous figure in American literature at that time."

Though comparison between authors is often as futile as it is fussy, the world of readers does not enthrone a man or a book without some conscious or unconscious correlation of his merits and his limitations with the merits and limitations of others. All our processes of perception and of reasoning are necessarily relative. And therefore it is that, in view

Edgar Allan Poe

of his aim, his method, and his success, in many lands and in a dozen languages, Poe remains, after half a century, the most broadly conspicuous of American writers. To call him the greatest is impossible,—the word " great " brings up ideas disconnected with his name,—but his intense star shines highest in our literary sky.

Upon what does this renown depend ? To a certain extent, undoubtedly, upon his personality, which, in itself and in its battles within and without, possessed something of the fascination wrought by that of a Heine, a Chopin, or, in a more blatant way, a Byron. It is not necessary to retell the tale of his short life, or to rake the embers of hateful fires of controversy. The son of strolling players, an adopted orphan, a spoiled child, a wayward but brilliant student, a literary hack, in his short career of forty years— often years of bitter poverty—he " hitched his wagon to a star " as truly as did the favored Emerson in his sheltered nook. His life was as chaste as his writings; he was the centre of a little home in which he was the idol of his young wife and her mother, toward both of whom his relations were tender; his intense ambition did not in itself color his view of the world, though the tone of increasing regret for things past re-echoes through much of his verse. For the rest, he was not addicted to the use of opium; he yielded too often, and fatally at last, to alcoholic excess; and his haughty aloofness of mind sometimes degenerated into selfish ingratitude. None of these things, however, affected the character of his work; and none, in a sense, is the reader's business. " Out of space, out of time," says a sage critic, is Poe's true epitaph. He, the uncanny dreamer, the child of sin and sorrow, was perpetually sane.

The personal appearance of the poet was striking and individual, according to all testimony. " A compact, well-set man about five feet six inches high, straight as an arrow, easy-gaited, with white linen coat and trousers, black velvet vest and Panama hat, features sad, yet finely cut, shapely head, and eyes that were strangely magnetic as you looked into them— this is the image of Edgar Allan Poe most vivid to my mind as I saw him one day in Richmond in 1849. There was a fascination about him that everybody felt. Meeting him in the midst of thousands a stranger would stop to get a second look, and to ask, ' Who is he ? ' " recalls Bishop O. P. Fitzgerald.[1] Mrs. Frances Sargent Osgood wrote, three years earlier,

---

[1] Professor J. A. Harrison's *New Glimpses of Poe*, 51.

to Miss Barrett (Mrs. Browning) that she ought to go to New York only to see his eyes flash through tears as he read her verses. As regards his voice, Professor Basil L. Gildersleeve says that he has " retained the impression that he did not read very well; his voice was pleasant enough, but he emphasized the rhythm unduly, a failing common, I believe, to poets endowed with a keen sense of the music of their own verse,"— as has been said of Tennyson and Rossetti. Thomas Wentworth Higginson says that Poe read *Ligeia* before a Boston audience in a voice whose singular music he has never heard equalled.

I am permitted to quote from a private letter (March 3, 1899) from a lady who well remembers the poet: " A few months before Mr. Poe died he visited at my father's house. It was an event then, and since the Poe renaissance, as I think it may be called, my girlish memories of him seem still more precious. He at once became the standard by which I measured all other men; and to this day no one has ever seemed to me his equal in the *tout ensemble* which goes to the making of a perfect gentleman. His quiet elegance, his courtly manner, his musical voice and refined accent, his glorious head and wonderful eyes, made an impression which time does not efface. My

xxiv

brother, several years older than I, who looked at Mr. Poe without feeling the kind of fascination that a girl in her early teens would do, still says: 'He was the most complete gentleman I ever saw.' " The writer adds: " He did not look 'weary and world-worn' " (an expression applied to him in a magazine article).

Poe's personality has, indeed, so vividly descended through the years since his death that it has been made a sort of international standard of comparison. Says Guy de Maupassant, of Swinburne, in his introduction to Mourey's surprisingly effective French translation of the *Poems and Ballads :* " Il me fit l'effet d'une sorte d'Edgar Poe idéaliste et sensuel, avec une âme d'écrivain plus exaltée, plus dépravée, plus amoureuse de l'etrange et du monstreux, plus curieuse, chercheuse et évocatrice des raffinements subtils et anti-naturels de la vie et de l'idée que celle de l'américain simplement évocatrice de fantômes et de terreurs. . . . J'ai pensé en le regardant pour la première fois, à Edgar Poe."

One point more, with reference to the poet as man. I hardly see how a broader error could have been uttered concerning Poe than that he " has only shown what he might have done had he been true, instead of tragically untrue, to his art and to himself." Does not Mr. Goldwin Smith here confuse the man and the artist ? All literature can hardly show a better example of constant, loyal, painstaking, perhaps over-minute service of the goddess of creative beauty in art. It would be more nearly true to say that Poe endangered his renown by a verbal nicety which sometimes became fussiness; but even here his changes were almost always improvements. Take a single example. In the first published version of the story called *The Assignation* (1834), a world-famous lyric closed thus:

> " Now all my hours are trances,
>   And all my nightly dreams
>   Are where thy gray eye glances,
>   And where thy footstep gleams,
>   In what ethereal dances,
>   By what Italian streams.
>
> " Alas! for that accursed time
>   They bore thee o'er the billow,
>   From love to titled age and crime,
>   And an unholy pillow:
>   From me and from our misty clime
>   Where weeps the silver willow."

Had Poe himself applied to these stanzas the acid criticism he was so fond of devoting to the works of others, he would have been the first to say that " hours " was not a word antithetical to " nightly "; that " Italian " was an unfortunate adjective to apply to waters of paradise; and that the closing stanza is repulsive in its idea, cheap in its choice of words, and an anticlimax. As it stands, the poem closes with two lines perfect in every detail of thought and expression,—

> " In what ethereal dances,
>   By what eternal streams,"—

as inherently and perennially lovely as Wordsworth's

> " And hear the mighty waters rolling evermore,"—

because in both cases the utterly poetic conception is phrased in the only words that seem exquisitely fit.

But perhaps the most obvious illustration of the development of a poor little germ into a finished lyric is to be found in the comparison of *Imitation* in the 1827 volume, with the finally elaborated *Dream within a Dream.* Here is the incoherent version in the *Tamerlane* booklet:

> " A dark unfathomed tide
>   Of interminable pride,
>   A mystery and a dream
>   Should my early life seem;
>   I say that dream was fraught
>   With a wild and waking thought

xxvii

Edgar Allan Poe

Of beings that have been,
Which my spirit had not seen
Had I let them pass me by
With a dreaming eye!
Let none of earth inherit
That vision on my spirit;
Those thoughts I would control
As a spell upon his soul;
For that bright hope at last
And that light time have past,
And my worldly rest hath gone
With a sigh as it passed on;
I care not though it perish
With a thought I then did cherish."

Two intermediate and experimental forms followed in
1829 and 1831.   In the first Poe introduced the lines

" I am standing 'mid the roar
Of a weather-beaten shore."

In the second they became

" I was standing 'mid the roar
Of a wind-beaten shore,"

which still dissatisfied the poet; and the final version
was the flawless couplet

" I stand amid the roar
Of a surf-tormented shore,"

the whole being recast as

xxviii

A DREAM WITHIN A DREAM.

" Take this kiss upon the brow!
And in parting from you now,
Thus much let me avow:
You are not wrong who deem
That my days have been a dream;
Yet if hope has flown away
In a night or in a day,
In a vision or in none,
Is it therefore the less gone ?
All that we see or seem
Is but a dream within a dream.

" I stand amid the roar
Of a surf-tormented shore,
And I hold within my hand
Grains of the golden sand,
How few! yet how they creep
Through my fingers to the deep,
While I weep, while I weep!
O God! can I not grasp
Them with a tighter clasp ?
O God! can I not save
One from the pitiless wave ?
Is all that we see or seem
But a dream within a dream ? "

The public of readers naturally demands that a poem be self-interpretative, and cares little for the mechanism of the manuscript page; the end crowns the work. Poe may have been willing that it should be believed that he dashed off his best poems in single moods of inspiration; but a hundred illustrations could be cited from his verse and prose, in various stages of elaboration, to show that not even Tennyson filed and polished with such artistic care. Indeed, the myth of the " madman of genius " might as well be applied to the writer of the *Elegy in a Country Churchyard.* One more example must suffice. The third stanza of *Lenore* in *The Pioneer* for February, 1843, runs thus:

" Peccavimus!
  But rave not thus!
    And let the solemn song
  Go up to God so mournfully that she may feel no
        wrong!
      The sweet Lenore
      Hath ' gone before '
        With young hope at her side,
          And thou art wild
          For the dear child
      That should have been thy bride,
          For her, the fair
          And debonair,
            That now so lowly lies,
          The life still there
          Upon her hair,
            The death upon her eyes."

The abandonment of this *Beautiful Snow* arrangement, and the nature of the final revisions, may be seen by turning to the poem in question.

xxx

World-Author

When the young poet sent to the once important critic, John Neal, in 1829, an early version of the "Fairy-Land" poem, under the title of *Heaven,* Neal called it, in the correspondence department of his magazine, nonsense, but rather exquisite nonsense; adding that if Poe " would but do justice to himself he might make a beautiful and perhaps a magnificent poem," which the boy gratefully acknowledged as the very first words of encouragement he remembered to have heard, saying: "I am very certain that as yet I have not written either, but that I can I will take oath, if they will give me time." *Al Aaraaf,* he went on to say, had some good poetry and much extravagance, which he had not had time to throw away. The youth of twenty, after all, justly estimated his own powers, and is to be praised, not blamed, for his high belief in his destiny. In one sense, this buoyancy gave him a happy life; the servant of the ideal can never be miserable. Beginning as a rather weak echo of Shelley, it was through his own unswerving efforts that he attained, in world-literature, the place he sought.

Poe, who evoked new and strange melodies from that old lute, the English language, has left five important records of his opinions and methods in things

xxxi

poetic, useful in their time and interesting because of their source; and in one of them, *The Philosophy of Composition,* he has given, with some exaggeration of memory, an account of the mechanical elaboration of his most famous lyric. Certainly he was a master craftsman in both poetry and prose; indeed, his tales, by their extraordinary nicety and definiteness of workmanship, and by their obvious variety and interestingness, have contributed more broadly to his general fame than has the little book of his exquisite verse.

Turning to the general body of his writings, two of the four divisions may briefly be dismissed. Of the few miscellanies even the ambitious *Eureka,* from which he hoped so much, is now read only by editors and proof-readers. His literary criticisms are naturally retained in his collected product; but with the exception of the treatises on verse, they are neither better nor worse than the average book-reviews one finds in the magazines or newspapers of to-day. Poe wrote them as a regularly recurrent duty, and his literary executor bound them up with his more permanent work, therefore we have them still. Of the American authors discussed in the *Literati* series and elsewhere, none have present rank or interest save

xxxii

World-Author

Hawthorne, Cooper, Longfellow, Lowell, and Bryant, or, in a lesser way, Halleck, Simms, Margaret Fuller, and Bayard Taylor. Among English writers he discussed Lever, Marryat, Dickens, Macaulay, and Mrs. Browning. The general tone of his criticism was sharp, or at least frank, save in the case of a few poets, minor or major, whom he overestimated and overpraised. One of his biographers speaks of " the literati that fell into Poe's clutches "; while another American critic alludes to the " series of papers on plagiarism, with their acuteness, their ostentation of learning, and their malice," which " was trailing through the *Mirror* and the *Broadway Journal."* Poe's first opinions of Longfellow were favorable; he had written to the Cambridge poet, May 3, 1841: " I cannot refrain from availing myself of this, the only opportunity I may ever have, to assure the author of the *Hymn to the Night,* of *The Beleaguered City,* and of *The Skeleton in Armor,* of the fervent admiration with which his genius has inspired me; and yet I would scarcely hazard a declaration whose import might be so easily misconstrued, and which bears with it, at best, more or less of *niaiserie,* were I not convinced that Professor Longfellow, writing and thinking as he does, will be at no loss to feel and to appreciate the honest sincerity of what I say "; and Longfellow had replied : "All that I have read from your pen has inspired me with a high idea of your power; and I think you are destined to stand among the first romance-writers of the country, if such be your aim." A few years later came the violent article entitled " Mr. Longfellow and Other Plagiarists," the most famous of all Poe's criticisms, of which the gentle author of *Evangeline* subsequently said to William Winter: " My works seemed to give him much trouble, first and last; but Mr. Poe is dead and gone, and I am alive and still writing, and that is the end of the matter. I never answered Mr. Poe's attacks; and I would advise you now, at the outset of your literary life, never to take notice of any attacks that may be made upon you. Let them all pass." Longfellow then took up a volume of Poe, and, turning the leaves, particularly commended *For Annie* and *The Haunted Palace.*

It seems singular that Poe should have so constantly insisted upon " the sin of plagiarism " (as he called it in the introduction to his 1845 volume of poems) in others, when falling into dubious situations himself. Thus he pointed out certain not very remarkable similarities between Hawthorne's *Howe's Masquerade*

xxxiv

and his own *William Wilson,* and between Longfellow's *Midnight Mass for the Dying Year* and Tennyson's *Death of the Old Year,* but himself gravely signed two prefaces to the first and second editions of *The Conchologist's First Book: a System of Testaceous Malacology,* by Edgar A. Poe, the subject being one on which he certainly had no first-hand knowledge; while in his *Tale of the Ragged Mountains* he paraphrased Macaulay, and in *The Journal of Julius Rodman* was indebted to Irving. Mr. Henry Austin (in *Literature* for August 4, 1899) has applied the " deadly parallel " to the *Tale of the Ragged Mountains* (1844) and Macaulay's *Essay on Warren Hastings* (1841) as follows:

MACAULAY.

" It was commonly believed that half a million of human beings were crowded into that labyrinth of lofty alleys, rich with shrines and minarets and balconies and carved oriels, to which the sacred apes clung by hundreds. The traveller could scarcely make his way through the press of holy

POE.

" On every hand was a wilderness of balconies, of verandas, of minarets, of shrines and fantastically carved oriels. . . . Besides these things were seen on all sides banners and palanquins, litters with stately dames closeveiled, elephants gorgeously caparisoned, idols grotesquely hewn, drums,

xxxv

352

mendicants and not less holy bulls.

. . . . . .

"The burning sun, the strange vegetation of the palm and the cocoa tree, the rice field, the tank, the huge trees, older than the Mogul empire, under which the village crowds assemble, the thatched roof of the peasant's hut . . . the drums, the banners and gaudy idols, the devotees swinging in the air, the graceful maiden with her pitcher on her head descending the steps to the riverside, etc."

banners and gongs, spears, silver and gilded maces. And amid the crowd and the clamor and the general intricacy and confusion—amid the million of black and yellow men, turbaned and robed and of flowing beard, there roamed a countless multitude of holy filleted bulls, while vast legions of the filthy but sacred ape clambered chattering and shrieking about the cornices of the mosques and clung to the minarets and oriels.

"Beyond the limits of the city arose in frequent and majestic groups the palm and the cocoa, with other gigantic and weird trees of vast age; and here and there might be seen a field of rice, the thatched hut of a peasant, a tank, a stray temple, a gypsy camp, or a solitary graceful maiden taking her way with a pitcher upon her head to the banks of the magnificent river."

xxxvi

World-Author

Certainly the residence of the author of the fierce essay on " Mr. Longfellow and Other Plagiarists " was somewhat vitreous; but what of it ? the definition of plagiarism has constantly been broadened since Shakespeare's day. If Poe is not an original author none ever lived; yet he might have been more charitable in regard to coincidences, unconscious repetitions, and legitimate reproductions.

But, after all, " malice " is a hard word to apply to Poe's method. His reviews, with all their faults of pettiness and whimsical opinionativeness, were at least honest and frankly helpful in a time when American " literary criticism " was sadly in need of breadth and perspective. Poe showed constant courage in not frequently yielding to the prevalent and still evident fashion of log-rolling and exchange of puffery; he did not promote his personal welfare, but rather stood in his own way, at a time when there was not much choice between the *Blackwood* slashing notice, and the saccharine laudation of some little local " poetess." For the rest, Poe's estimates were sometimes prophetically just; and he was not far from later opinions—Swinburne's, for instance—in declaring that " Miss Barrett has done more, in poetry, than any woman, living or dead." Elsewhere, in the well-known dedication of the 1845 poems, he called her " the noblest of her sex," which led her to say to John Kenyon: " What is to be said, I wonder, when a man calls you the ' noblest of your sex ' ? ' Sir, you are the most discerning of yours.' " To Robert Browning she wrote at greater length, early in the following year:

" I send you besides a most frightful extract from an American magazine sent to me yesterday . . . on the subject of mesmerism; and you are to understand, if you please, that the Mr. Edgar Poe who stands committed to it, is my dedicator, . . . whose dedication I forgot, by the way, with the rest, —so, while I am sending, you shall have his poems with his mesmeric experience and decide whether the outrageous compliment to E. B. B. or the experiment on M. Vandeleur [Valdemar] goes furthest to prove him mad. There is poetry in the man, though, now and then, seen between the great gaps of bathos. . . . *Politian* will make you laugh, as *The Raven* made me laugh, though with something in it which accounts for the hold it took upon people such as Mr. N. P. Willis and his peers; it was sent to me from four different quarters besides the author himself, before its publication in this form, and when it had only a newspaper life. Some of the other lyrics have power of a less questionable sort. For the author, I do not know him at all,—never heard from him nor wrote to him,—and in my opinion, there is more faculty shown in the account of that horrible mesmeric experience (mad or not mad) than in his poems. Now do read

xxxviii

it from the beginning to the end. That ' going out ' of the hectic, struck me very much . . . and the writing away of the upper lip. Most horrible! Then I believe so much of mesmerism as to give room for the full acting of the story on me . . . without absolutely giving full credence to it, understand ? "

In his criticism of Miss Barrett occurs a passage of importance when we think of Poe's own apparent relations to Shelley and Coleridge, whom he had imitated in *Tamerlane* and *Al Aaraaf*, and his esteem for Tennyson. He speaks admiringly of Shelley's impulsive bird-songs for the mere joy of his own song; deplores the " preposterously anomalous metaphysicianism " of Coleridge; and declares that Miss Barrett narrowly escaped uniting " the Shelleyan abandon, the Tennysonian poetic sense, the most profound instinct of art, and the sternest will properly to blend and vigorously to control all "—which may be taken as Poe's own ideal creed for the poet.

In the notice of Hawthorne, furthermore, is a similar passage of so great illustrative value that it is worth the aggregate of the rest of the criticisms, for it sets forth the views of one of the two American masters of the short story, on the basis of an examination of some of the writings of the other.

" The tale proper, in my opinion," says Poe, " affords

xxxix

Edgar Allan Poe

unquestionably the fairest field for the exercise of the loftiest talent which can be afforded by the wide domains of mere prose. . . . I need only here say, upon this topic, that, in almost all classes of composition, the unity of effect or impression is a point of the greatest importance. It is clear, moreover, that this unity cannot be thoroughly preserved in productions whose perusal cannot be completed at one sitting. . . . All high excitements are necessarily transient. Thus a long poem is a paradox. And, without unity of impression, the deepest effects cannot be brought about. . . . Without a certain continuity of effort, without a certain duration or repetition of purpose, the soul is never deeply moved. . . . Were I called upon, however, to designate that class of composition which, next to such a poem as I have suggested, should best fulfil the demands of high genius, should offer it the most advantageous field of exertion, I should unhesitatingly speak of the prose tale, as Mr. Hawthorne has here exemplified it. I allude to the short prose narrative, requiring from a half-hour to one or two hours in its perusal. The ordinary novel is objectionable, from its length, for reasons already stated in substance. As it cannot be read at one sitting, it deprives itself, of course, of the immense force derivable from totality. . . . In the brief tale, however, the author is enabled to carry out the fulness of his intention, be it what it may. During the hour of perusal the soul of the reader is at the writer's control. . . .

" A skilful literary artist has constructed a tale. If wise, he has not fashioned his thoughts to accommodate his incidents; but having conceived, with de-

xl

liberate care, a certain unique or single effect to be
wrought out, he then invents such incidents, he then
combines such events, as may best aid him in estab-
lishing this preconceived effect. If his very initial
sentence tend not to the outbringing of this effect,
then he has failed in his first step. In the whole
composition there should be no word written of which
the tendency, direct or indirect, is not to the one pre-
established design. And by such means, with such
care and skill, a picture is at length painted which
leaves in the mind of him who contemplates it with
a kindred art, a sense of the fullest satisfaction. The
idea of the tale has been presented unblemished, be-
cause undisturbed; and this is an end unattainable
by the novel. Undue brevity is just as exceptionable
here as in the poem; but undue length is yet more
to be avoided. . . .

"The tale has a point of superiority even over the
poem. In fact, while the rhythm of this latter is an
essential aid in the development of the highest idea—
the idea of the beautiful—the artificialities of this
rhythm are an insuperable bar to the development of
all points of thought or expression which have their
basis in truth. But truth is often, and in very great
degree, the aim of the tale. Some of the finest tales
are tales of ratiocination. Thus the field of this
species of composition, if not so elevated a region on
the mountain of mind, is a table-land of far vaster
extent than the domain of the mere poem. Its prod-
ucts are never so rich, but infinitely more numerous,
and more appreciable by the mass of mankind. The
writer of the prose tale, in short, may bring to his
theme a vast variety of modes or inflections of thought

xii

and expression (the ratiocinative, for example, the sarcastic, or the humorous) which are not only antagonistical to the nature of the poem, but absolutely forbidden by one of its most peculiar and indispensable adjuncts; we allude, of course, to rhythm. It may be added here, *par parenthèse,* that the author who aims at the purely beautiful in a prose tale is laboring at a great disadvantage; for beauty can be better treated in a poem."

Everybody knows his statement that " poetry has only collateral relations with the intellect and the conscience, and, unless incidentally, no concern whatever with either duty or truth "; fewer recall his equally confident assertion, in this Hawthorne critique, that, under the best circumstances, allegory " must always interfere with that unity of effect which, to the artist, is worth all the allegory in the world." . . . " *The Pilgrim's Progress* is a ludicrously overrated book." But the short stories of Hawthorne (of which he was speaking in the remark just quoted) clearly disprove his dictum; and in his own *William Wilson* he builded better than he knew.

The primacy of the American short story has certainly been due, in large part, to Poe's insistence that it be a unit and leave on the mind a definite result. His own tales, on the whole, may be said to have

xlii

constituted and created a new *genre.* There had been realists, from Chaucer to Defoe; and the German and French waves of romanticism had unquestionably affected the continental prose tale,—not a very important thing in itself. But to call Poe's work " Hoffmannesque " is like the old application of the term " Gothic " to everything not Italian. " All that flams is not flamboyant," nor is all weirdness imitative. Out of the stock properties of the horrible and the uncanny Poe created a result as unlike Hoffmann's as *Lady Eleanore's Mantle* is unlike *Robinson Crusoe.* It is much for a national literature, within the same half-century, to have added two such writers as Poe and Hawthorne—like and yet profoundly unlike—to the library of the world.

The best tales of Poe fall naturally into several somewhat marked divisions: of the dread battle of life and death (*Ligeia, The Fall of the House of Usher*); of ratiocination (*The Gold Bug, The Murders in the Rue Morgue, The Mystery of Marie Rogêt, The Purloined Letter*); of the borderland between science and imagination (*The Balloon-Hoax, MS. Found in a Bottle, The Facts in the Case of M. Valdemar*); of morals (*The Black Cat, The Tell-Tale Heart, The Man of the Crowd William Wilson*); of cumulative horror (*The*

xliii

Edgar Allan Poe

Pit and the Pendulum); of humor (*The System of Professor Tarr and Doctor Fether, The Man that was Used up*). These divisions run into each other and may be altered by various readers, or by the same reader in his variant moods. All the stories mentioned, in their several ways, are masterpieces of clear thought, definite construction, unswerving progress toward the end proposed. Their analytic method and their imaginative power coincide in a way not elsewhere to be found in the literature of the world. If " the heart somehow seems all squeezed out by the mind,"—if they are markedly inferior to the stories of Hawthorne in deep probing of the problems of the human soul, they are superior, on the whole, in intensity of instant effect.

Poe did not, as has been said of Chaucer, " transmute swarming humanity into a few symbolic types "; but there is a world elsewhere. If any moral tendency inheres in the evolution of human society, it inheres in such pictures of that society as Chaucer and Shakespeare, for instance, give us. But simpler things— wonder, horror, surprise, motion, color—please not less, and have their place in art. Poe was no promoter of piety, patriotism, gentle friendship, love of animals, and what may be termed the minor affections

xliv

which play a larger part than stressful moods in most lives; yet it is as true as ever that, in the words of the Latin maxim, we cannot all of us do all things. He was certainly a narrow worker, but it is idle to assert that the author of *William Wilson,* one of the great allegories of conscience, divorced art from ethics. The limner of death was what he was because he insisted that death must yield to the forceful self-assertion of a quenchless soul. If Poe's soul is not existent at this moment, the universe is, in Whitman's vigorous putting of the matter, " a suck and a sell."

Being a man, Poe was compelled to portray humanity against a worldly background, and there are, of course, local touches or tints in his stories: of the Ragged Mountains near his university, of the London school of his boyhood, of India, of Sullivan's Island in Charleston harbor, etc.; but with all his nice realism he wrote few " tales of a time and a place." His visualized trees and tarns, his mansions and corridors and darksome rooms, are of the land east of the sun and west of the moon, not of Philadelphia or New York or old-world localities made familiar to him in his reading. Names of American scenes or newspapers appear under various disguises in *The Mystery of Marie Rogêt,* but their import is universal. The Rue Morgue may

xlv

Edgar Allan Poe

seem like a Paris thoroughfare, but it is still more a lane in the large world. He treated things and events between 1809 and 1849 as Botticelli treated his Italy; and his physical universe is as symbolic as the figures and fruits and flowers of the Primavera. The minutest of artists in delicate detail, it seems impossible to connect him with the century of the railway and the telegraph—wireless telegraphy, which he was capable of inventing, would have been more to his liking.

As regards the charge that Poe was a mere mechanician, a sufficient reply is that the effect of his tales remains in the spirit more than in the mind. The creator of Sherlock Holmes has frankly called that personage " merely a mechanical creature," not a man of flesh and blood; and " easy to create because he was soulless. One story by Edgar Allan Poe would be worth a dozen such." To Dr. Doyle, Poe's creations are evidently not mere automata, or their creator " fantastically inhuman," as he has been termed. A French critic notes dryness as a mark of Poe's stories; to others this same quality appears the deliberateness of art. Indeed, some of his stories are " too strange not to be true." His " Racconti Incredibili," as the Italians call them, now and then reappear in the real world. Poe, like Charles Reade, knew that the an-

xlvi

nals of actual life afford the best illustrations of the impossible.

Though a master of grotesquerie, Poe was deficient in true humor and in its concomitant pathos. In the former his chief achievement is *The System of Doctor Tarr and Professor Fether,* amusing, but certainly not a masterpiece; as regards the latter, the feelings he arouses, in his prose, stop short of " the tender grace of a day that is dead."

Perhaps he most narrowly escaped failure in the " prose-poems," where his art was nearest the surface. *Silence,* with its weak repetitiousness, suggests the feebleness of decadent iteration rather than the mastery of alliteration, of assonance, of an essentially Hebrew parallelism, which we find in his onomatopoetic verse at its best. But in his titles he often attained perfection: who can change such verbal collocations as *The Island of the Fay, The Murders in the Rue Morgue, The Masque of the Red Death, The Imp of the Perverse, The Fall of the House of Usher,* which are poems in themselves.

And what new thing shall we say of the verse, concerning which so many words have been uttered by so many men ? Criticism is not indispensable, for true poetry is as self-explanatory as a bird-song or a gem.

xlvii

Edgar Allan Poe

Thousands have enjoyed the melody of *The Bells;* thousands have been touched by the melancholy of *The Raven.* Poe, says John Sartain, the veteran engraver, " was naturally modest, but one day, while laboring under the influence of drink, he said to Thomas Buchanan Read: ' Read, say what they will, I have written one poem that shall live forever—*The Raven.'"* Scarcely less familiar are the figures of Lenore or Annabel Lee, sweeping mystically from the hitherto to the hereafter. The undefinable mystery of *The City in the Sea, The Sleeper, The Valley of Unrest, The Conqueror Worm,* or the overpraised *Haunted Palace* has made for itself a niche in the temple of fame. Mr. Lang has well spoken of " that undefinable quality of the rare, the strange, the hitherto unheard, yet delightful note which now and again is heard in the verse of Edgar Poe. . . . Not his ideas, but the beauty of his haunting lines confers on him the laurel." His poems, known by English readers in their own dialect, transferred line for line and almost word for word into the similar German, not wholly lost even when transmuted into French prose, occupy a place that is unique.

We need not, in considering Poe's verse, any more than in his prose, trouble ourselves with discussions of real or supposed " precursors," from *Kubla Khan* to Pike's *Isidore,* or the verbal concoctions of Thomas Holley Chivers. The similarities between Tennyson and Keats, or between Swinburne and Tennyson, which no one would think of elaborating, are really more numerous than the relations between Poe and his fellows on the modest slopes of the American Parnassus. He lived and wrote in a sentimental and romantic period, when the ideas and the phraseology of verse were rapidly and sometimes foolishly expanding. What he invented was indubitably his own; what little he found or adapted he stamped with his individuality. His pet words—" Lenore," " Ulalume," " Israfel," " naphthaline," " nevermore," etc.—are peculiarly his; and when, a hundred and fifty years earlier, we find in Dryden such lines as

" See the Furies arise!
  See the snakes that they rear,
  How they hiss in their hair,
  And the sparkles that flash from their eyes!
  Behold a ghastly band,
  Each a torch in his hand!
  Those are Grecian ghosts, that in battle were slain,
  And unburied remain
  Inglorious on the plain,"

xlix

Edgar Allan Poe

we merely say that there was a Poesque touch in *Alexander's Feast.* The most tangible influence upon him is of course Mrs. Browning's atrocious-admirable *Lady Geraldine's Courtship, passim,* and especially the line,

" With a murmurous stir uncertain, in the air the
      purple curtain ";

but every one who has written verse or composed music knows the impossibility of dissevering inventions from remembered phrases. Those inclined to concern themselves with Poe " parallels " would better spend their time in reading Thomas Lovell Beddoes, an incarnation, as unquestionable as original, of a spirit akin to his.

Tone-color in English verse, and not less truly in French, became a different and a more apparent thing after Poe had lived and sung. From Pope to Poe— the difference between classicism and romanticism is but the loss of a letter. Coleridge, Poe, Rossetti, Swinburne, the Paris symbolists—the order of influence is only less marked than the order of time. But there are great differences between him and his admiring successors. It is an error to call Poe soulless, non-ethical, pagan, a man of morbid taste,

1

anrelated to the great problems of source, life, and destiny. That he was no polemic; that he was indifferent to the great ethical movements of his time; that he was ever the apostle of beauty; and that he could not have written Wordsworth's *Ode on Immortality* or Emerson's *Terminus,* is clear. It is interesting to note that from a French, not an Anglo-Saxon, critic comes the declaration that " on cherchait vainement, dans ses écrits, cette harmonie sereine qui caracterise les véritables chefs-d'œuvre." [1] But in one thing his name must rank high in the spiritual movements of his time and of all time: his insistence upon the earned perpetuity of personal assertion. The individual will live because it wills to live, that is his gospel from first to last. *Annabel Lee,* not less than Browning's *Prospice,* is the quintessence of belief in the two things which are the final hopes and claims of spiritual religion: personality, and a source of all things which creates the love to reward the love.

" If the doctrine of the indestructibility of individuality be a delusion, Poe must hold rank as the most logical and most convincing of dreamers. If there be such a thing in men, or in any man, as an

---

[1] B. Ernouf, *Revue Contemporaine,* juillet, 1862.

lj

Edgar Allan Poe

immortal soul, Poe must be accounted one of its noblest, although unordained, proclaimers and priests. In others of his graver stories one could point out the metaphysical and religious value of his contributions to the cause of reasoned spirituality, now meeting an organized pressure from the ranks of a crass and scientifically bigoted materialism, and could easily show what a large debt is owing to this long-abused and imperfectly understood artist by that conservative portion of society which has been absurdly taught to regard him as an Ishmaelite, chiefly because in his latest adventure amid the ' Ragged Mountains ' of this world Poe, the man, so often fell by the wayside.[1] Or if I may quote my own words in a previous essay: ' The will dieth not; God himself is but a great will; man by the strength of will conquers death that conquers all else. This is the answer to the riddle of Poe, and to the vaster enigma of this world.' "

It may be added that Poe stands supreme, even in the only morally pure national literature the world has ever seen, in the absolute chastity of his every word.

The ideal vision of pure beauty, now incarnate and now but a mist-figure, pallid or rosy, ever floated before the poet's eyes. It hypnotized him like a crystal ball. To it he addressed the shorter lyric *To Helen,* most perfect of all his poems. *Annabel Lee*

---

[1] Henry Austin, *Literature,* August 4, 1899.

lii

369

was not only the song of a single loss, but a passionate world-cry of the immortal to the immortal. Past *One in Paradise* flow the eternal streams. If Poe's assertive belief in the immortality of the soul of beauty sometimes veered toward the mood of despair, we must not forget that to every man, at times, death seems death indeed, and the door of the tomb appears open to receive those who pass into the dreamless sleep, with never a hint of release or renewal:

> " Not all the preaching since Adam
> Has made death other than death."

But he who finds in this thought the last word of the author of *The Raven* has never read his other and greater poems at all. It is more than a coincidence that, in the chronological arrangement of his verse, the final words are:

> " ' Down the valley of the shadow,
>   Ride, boldly ride,'
>   The Shade replied,
> ' If you seek for Eldorado! ' "

CHARLES F. RICHARDSON.

DARTMOUTH COLLEGE,
    March 1, 1902.

liii